Through Ebby's

Eyes

A Powerful, True Story
—Told from a Dog's Perspective

Lori Ellen Brochhagen

BALBOA.
PRESS
A DIVISION OF HAY HOUSE

Balboa Press books may be ordered through booksellers or by contacting:

Balboa Press
A Division of Hay House
1663 Liberty Drive
Bloomington, IN 47403
www.balboapress.com
1 (877) 407-4847

Because of the dynamic nature of the Internet, any web addresses or
links contained in this book may have changed since publication and
may no longer be valid. The views expressed in this work are solely those
of the author and do not necessarily reflect the views of the publisher,
and the publisher hereby disclaims any responsibility for them.

The author of this book does not dispense medical advice or prescribe the use
of any technique as a form of treatment for physical, emotional, or medical
problems without the advice of a physician, either directly or indirectly. The
intent of the author is only to offer information of a general nature to help
you in your quest for emotional and spiritual well-being. In the event you use
any of the information in this book for yourself, which is your constitutional
right, the author and the publisher assume no responsibility for your actions.

Any people depicted in stock imagery provided by Thinkstock are models,
and such images are being used for illustrative purposes only.
Certain stock imagery © Thinkstock.

Print information available on the last page.

ISBN: 978-1-5043-6789-9 (sc)
ISBN: 978-1-5043-6791-2 (hc)
ISBN: 978-1-5043-6790-5 (e)

Library of Congress Control Number: 2016916768

Balboa Press rev. date: 10/28/2016

For Joshua

You grew from a bright-eyed child, full of joy for life and unjudging compassion for others—into a man who possesses integrity with himSelf and with the Universe. You amaze me with your courage and grace; you make me grin with your honesty and humor. My heart beats with gratitude and joy—because, I get to be your mom.

CONTENTS

CHAPTER ONE

*M*mm ... she smelled so good. And she said she'd be back! People say that a lot as they back out the door to the shelter; I suppose it's because they feel bad about leaving us in these cages.

Most people do not return, but I knew this lady was coming back, just by the way she looked at me when she said it. Her eyes were bright green that day; they sometimes change from green to blue, but that day they were definitely green. And they were rimmed with red. I could smell the tears on her breath when she sat on the floor of my pen and hugged me. I smelled something else, too. It felt good, but I didn't have a word for it; the aroma made me think of comforting things--like belly rubs and food.

We both needed rescuing; I from this cage, and she from the desperate hopelessness that I could sense that was crushing her.

Last month I was a five-month-old puppy, basking in the love of a little girl and her family--well, most of the family. The father smelled bad; his breath reeked of stale alcohol and something festering deep inside. Most evenings he would yell, so my little girl and I would hide in her closet until he went to sleep. One evening he was angrier and louder than ever before and his voice roared through the house. The next day they put all their things in boxes. My little girl was crying and I couldn't comfort her like I usually could; this time she was inconsolable. But no one would listen to her; they just shoved her into the back seat of the car. He scooted me out onto the porch as he locked the front door and joined the rest of the family in the car; the engine roared--and they left.

I sat on the porch like a good pup, waiting for them to get back. I think a part of me knew they weren't going to return; I could sense that it was different than when they left me to go to the store. I had to wait, though. At night I was cold and kind of scared; all kinds of animals come out when humans go to bed. Also, I was getting pretty hungry and thirsty, but I waited. What else was I to do? They were my family.

On the third day, some people came to the house; they patted my head, gave me water, and said, "poor doggie." Then one of the ladies took me to jail.

The north coast of California rarely sees thunderstorms, yet during my first night in jail one of these odd, exhilarating storms occurred and another dog, an Airedale and Irish wolfhound mix named Luna, ignored her human's pleas for her to return and romped off into the bushes as the rain soaked through the thick undercoat of her fur.

As the lightening flashed, the kennel door opened and one of the girls walked in and placed a small ball of fur on the floor of one of the pens. She spoke softly as she toweled it dry; then she got up, latched the gate and left the kennel. As soon as the door shut the little fur-ball started making a lot of noise, yipping and whining like crazy; he was pretty distraught.

This little thing couldn't have weighed more than eight pounds. He shook continuously and every time he spoke his whole body jumped. He said his name was Manuel, but that everyone called him

Manny. He told us about a friend of his, named Luna, that had been killed that evening, how they were all running around and playing together and how the storm came on suddenly.

Sometimes we just can't help it; we hear our humans pleading with us to return, but something primal takes over--and we just have to run. That night, with the whipping wind bringing stinging rain, and the crashing and flashing of the thunder and lightening, apparently, Luna couldn't stop either; I bet it was awesome! Manny told us that she spotted the deer and that was it, there was no way she could *not* chase it. She bolted through the field of the apartment complex, quickly gaining on the buck; when he realized how close she was, he sprang into action and the chase was on. The buck had told the little trembling dog that he enjoyed this play, knowing they could never reach him. Luna had chased him before; she was the fastest in this neighborhood but even she couldn't catch him. He had crossed this part of the road many times; it was dark and the absence of headlights told him he could do it safely. And he did.

Yet there *was* a car; and it was traveling far too fast in the wet weather, and for some reason it's headlights were off as it sped through the neighborhood. The little dog told us he started barking at Luna because he had seen the car; he tried to get her to stop, but the roar of the storm covered his pleas.

The buck made it safely. Had Luna been one second faster--just *one* second--she would have made it also. He turned in time to see her black body land in a pile of leaves and lie motionless, long wet hair splayed around her. Manny and the buck's eyes met, and they both knew a little boy and a lady with green eyes just lost their best friend.

That storm changed *all* of our lives. A week later the lady with the bright green eyes and red hair came into the jail. She walked into the room full of pens; mine was first in the row. I grabbed my toy and sat at my gate wagging my tail, looking as happy and adorable as I could. Although, I was still having difficulty mastering that soulful look that so many humans seem to like. She smiled at me ...

then kept walking. My heart sank. I usually get passed by; I'm just a plain black dog, but I keep hoping.

She rounded the room, stopping and greeting each of the other prisoners. Once she had seen us all she came back--to me! Now, I wriggled my whole body excitedly. *Please, please ...*

The lady walked up to my pen, opened the gate and came in. She bent over to say hello, extending her hand so I could smell her. I didn't need to smell any more to know I wanted her to take me home. Oh, I was so excited. *Don't pee on her* was all I could think. She sat herself down on my cell floor and let me come to her, which I did with glee. I got as close as I could, sat down and put my head against her chest, snuggling into the crook of her neck as tightly as I was able.

She chuckled and hugged me, "Oh, you are such a sweetie. How could anyone leave you?"

Then she rose, stepped outside the gate and latched it. The lady looked at me and said, "I'm coming back." She said it firmly and with such sincerity, not at all like the others say it.

When the kennel door shut behind her little Manny started yipping at me.

"That's her! That's her!" His body jumped an inch off the floor with each bark, "Hey, you! Lab down at the end there, that's her! That's Luna's human!"

Two hours later, the girl at the jail came back to get me--I thought for my walk, except we went out a different door. That was her scent! She *did* come back! Once I got to her she bent down to pet me; in my excitement I knocked her off balance and she landed, hard, on her hind quarters. I flinched, expecting to be reprimanded. But when I opened my eyes, I could see her laughing. Oh, I am never leaving this green-eyed woman's side. Not ever.

Arriving at my new home, I met the two other humans that I had smelled on her clothing. One, which I liked right away, was her son. He was a blue-eyed blonde boy of about ten years; he felt like a good boy, and he also smelled like tears. Yet he was very friendly and readily welcomed me with lots of hugs.

The other one--the husband but not the boy's father--smelled like my little girl's father so I was wary. Instinct said to snarl; however, I knew on some level, that if this human didn't like me--well, I wouldn't get to stay. I just needed to win him over. When he first saw me he grimaced and threw up his hands.

"Of all the dogs to get--you know I don't like that kind of dog, short-haired, black, tail between the legs. She looks whiny." He shook his head, giving the lady a look that made her tense up, and walked away.

When we got inside the house, I sat and waited for my moment. Then, as he walked toward the kitchen doorway, I stood in front of him and looked him in the eye; he stopped and looked back.

"What?"

I lifted myself up and put my front paws on his chest, maintaining eye contact and wagging my tail ever so slightly. He laughed.

To the lady he said, "Oh, she's good," and to me, "Okay, you win. Well-played, dog."

Ye-es!

At the shelter, they had named me Angel. The green-eyed lady didn't like it, saying she knew too many dogs with that name. She looked at me for a long time, considering several options and discarding them.

"Ebony. That's her name. Ebony," she stated with certainty. I found out, years later, that I am named after her aunt's cat. A *cat*.

The lady, *my* lady, and I fit together perfectly; she says she doesn't think it's right to train animals to perform, either for humans' entertainment or for obedience sake. *And,* as luck would have it, I happen to be an *incredibly* intelligent, intuitive canine. She talks to me as she would to another human, and I almost always get what she means. There are no words like, "heal, sit, stay or beg" between us. I hear things like, "Wait a minute," and I know to stop walking. "That's really unattractive," means to stop begging. And, "Ew, gross Ebby!" means I should stop licking myself.

****

CHAPTER TWO

My lady and I frequently went into town, to take our boy to the school bus stop, to get food, and talk to people while the man stayed home. He liked to listen to the radio, smoke cigarettes, drink coffee and scribble furiously in his notebook. Sometimes he went out, but he didn't smell of sweat or have the weariness of labor on him when he returned. He still just smelled like cigarettes and coffee. The man did make dinner most nights, and my little boy would always try to feed it to me under the table; there was never any meat in it and it always contained something green, so as much as I wanted to help him out, it really held no interest for me.

There were times when her husband smelled strongly of alcohol, like he did when I first came to my new home. Along with the alcohol, there was another, ever-present odor--one that humans never seem to notice. It can be likened to rotting meat, I suppose--as if something were festering inside his body.

When he drank he would yell back at the radio or turn up the music loud enough to be painful for me and he would dance, and he would break things. Those were the times I made myself as small as I could, in a corner somewhere, so as not to get stepped on; and those were the times when he'd hurt my lady. But I never knew what to do because I didn't smell any fear from her; there was nothing. It was as though her body was empty, like she just went somewhere else and returned to a battered body when the violence was over. He didn't touch my little boy; he was mean sometimes and played too rough, but there was no blatant violence.

When I was almost a year old everything changed.

I could feel her increasing anxiety; she always seemed to be worried. She worked, but there never seemed to be enough food. She made sure to get her son to school early enough that he could get breakfast before classes started. Hand-washed clothes hung in front of the wood stove to dry. At night there were always candles burning, and on chilly mornings the oven door stood open as they huddled around it while drinking coffee and listening to the news on something called "Public Radio."

"One day you're going to interview me," my lady said to the blaring radio as she shoved items into a large backpack.

A few days earlier we had been in town, meeting with a group of people that we saw regularly. As a man across the room spoke, my lady sat there politely, but she was not listening. I could feel her anxiety as she stared past the man; she closed her eyes and breathed in through her nose and out through her mouth. Then suddenly, something he said jerked her back to the room.

"So I just decided to go for a long walk to clear my head," he said and was about to continue when my lady jumped in.

"That's it! I'm going to walk," she exclaimed as if everyone, instead of listening to the man, had been following the conversation in her head. When she realized she had spoken out loud, she slapped her hand over her mouth.

"I'm sorry. I'm so sorry," she spoke through her fingers.

She had difficulty standing still through the prayer they said in unison each time they met. They had barely finished chanting, "It works if you work it," before we were skipping down the stairs and out to the pick-up truck. I turned back and glimpsed the other members of the group staring after us, shaking their heads and shrugging their shoulders.

I could feel an excitement, like during a lightening storm with so much electricity in the air; the smell is exhilarating. Instead of the desperation she had been exuding, I felt hope--and determination.

Then one month later, we said goodbye to her son and her husband, and we started walking. I was confused. You didn't even have to be a dog to know how much she loved our boy. Yet she was leaving him with that man who smelled bad.

On the first day of our new adventure, March 20, 2003, we walked over fifteen miles; we walked down the coast road, then headed east when we got to Navarro Beach. That evening we slept at Paul Dimmick campground; it was still the off season so it was closed. By the time we had arrived, my lady was limping. However, she walked around until she found the perfect spot to settle in for the night, kind of like a dog would do; she's funny like that sometimes. She assembled the small tent, which was to be our shelter for the next six weeks, and made nice cozy beds for us both.

Her feet were bleeding when she removed her new hiking boots and the bandages she had applied earlier. I was starting to get a little tired, but I would have been ready for a few hours more walking after a short nap. We were barely fed before she fell soundly asleep until dawn. I was too excited to sleep, so I sat and watched over my lady with the green eyes, loving her and keeping her safe from all the night sounds.

This was a good place to sleep and there were plenty more to be enjoyed throughout our journey. The farther south and east we got, however, the more difficult it was to find such ideal resting places. So we learned what my lady called "guerilla camping." Sometimes we slept in drainage ditches, in abandoned houses or in the bushes on the side of a highway.

At first light we were up. After looking up and thanking the sky for "guiding and keeping us safe," she gave me some breakfast, brushed her teeth and hair and made sure we left nothing behind.

Her pack was hoisted onto her back, with a grunt and a little fart, and we were off again. For the next ten days, this was how it went. The next night we stayed in the Hendy campground, where there may still be a stash of almonds in a certain campsite. Through Philo and Booneville we walked along Highway 128 which was densely lined with redwoods. Sometimes my lady would twirl around, looking up at the green canopy, and laugh.

"Thank you, Spirit! You are such a great artist," she would exclaim as we watched the sun rise or set, or when she would see a particularly pretty grouping of trees or flowers.

Back on the coast it was a regular practice for residents to gather along the bluffs to watch the sun set on the ocean. Cars lined the Mendocino headlands; people listened to music or cuddled with loved ones, kids flew kites and, when the police were not patroling, dogs chased after frisbees, balls and low-flying seagulls. There were times when the light show was so spectacular and colorful that my lady would break into applause, others turned and looked at her, then joined in, hooting and whistling their appreciation to someone they called Mother Nature.

There wasn't much shoulder so she walked the white line and I walked to her right as when we heard a car horn tooting from behind us. It pulled ahead to where there was a turn-off and waited for us to get closer. The car held a couple of our friends from Mendocino, a young man with large brown eyes and long lashes and his father. When they were finished hugging and the men had sufficiently scratched my back they pulled a bag from the back seat of the car.

"Here, this might come in handy," the young man held out red plastic pants and a poncho.

"Rain gear! Oh, this is great; that's something I forgot; how did you know?" she grinned and asked as she was rolling it up so it would fit in her overstuffed backpack.

"It's what I forgot when I was hiking," the young man laughed.

"We were thinking that this might come in handy also." They both grinned as the father handed her a plastic jar full of sticky, skunky buds.

"Oh, you guys rock." She opened the jar and inhaled deeply. "Thank you so much!" We sat and chatted for a while, then the men did a u-turn and headed back to the coast as we headed on to Cloverdale.

On our fifth day of walking, we stopped for breakfast at a small diner that had a picture of an owl on it. My lady sat at a table by the window where she could look out at me as I sat with the pack. Afterward, she came out with a large meat patty that had been cooling while she ate.

Less than a half hour later it occurred to me that I might die. Surely that had to be what was happening to me. I had trouble standing and the earth beneath my feet seemed to be swaying. I was violently ill and threw up every few minutes, although my stomach had been purged of its contents with the first two heaves. After a while, exhaustion kept me from even getting up and being sick away from where I was laying.

My lady had tears in her eyes and she kept saying she was sorry; I wanted to comfort her but I hadn't the strength; I couldn't even see her clearly. As I lay in the driveway of a health food store, watching the world spin around me, she went inside. A few moments later she came out and was holding a white tablet, which she gently pushed down my throat with her finger as she held my head in her lap.

"Please be okay, Ebby," she whispered as she held me. Somehow, it stayed in my belly and I felt better almost right away. I did not vomit again, and the spinning world finally calmed down. There would be no more walking that day, though, I didn't feel *that* good.

A man came out of the store not long after I began to feel better.

"How's she doing," he asked as he bent down to pet me.

"Much better. That pill was amazing; I can't believe how quickly it worked! Thank you so much. She stopped getting sick as soon as I gave it to her," she exclaimed. I could sense the relief in her voice; then I could feel her anger and disbelief.

"We went over to the diner and I asked for a side of meat for her. Bitch gave her bad meat. Why would she do that?"

He shook his head as he glanced over toward the restaurant and said he was sorry.

"Some people," he muttered.

"Here, take some more of these to keep with you," he handed her a small bag of pills. "They're herbal; they won't hurt her. There are some for motion sickness and some for stress." Before he went back inside he told us about a place to camp.

"If the cops come, tell them I said it was okay to stay there for the night." As it turned out, the police did show up. I don't like the way they smell; there's something about them ... I can't help growling at them if they get too close. Once he saw that my lady had a tight grip on my collar, the officer was nice and, once she told him who referred us, he said there was no problem with us being there.

After that, there was no money, really; what little money my lady had in her pocket when we left the Mendocino Coast was gone. So the two of us drank water and ate trail mix and energy bars. I would always take the almonds out, like I did at the Hendy campground, and I'd bury them where we camped so that when the trail mix was gone we would still have the nuts. I buried the almonds because they are my favorites. However, we never seemed to return to where I had them buried, which means some little squirrel or chipmunk got them, I'm sure.

People would pass in cars and wave and beep; sometimes they would stop and ask us what we were doing. People commuting to and from work might see us a couple of days in a row as we walked through their towns. Sometimes they would stop.

One day a white-haired, wrinkled man stopped his car across the street from us.

"Hey! I've seen you walking for a couple of days. What are ya doin', anyway?" He yelled.

We crossed the street so she didn't have to raise her voice. Once my lady told him what we were up to, he smiled and started talking to her about having gone to a place called Vietnam. He talked for a few minutes, then thanked her for listening.

"I have family, but there are things I can't talk to them about," he paused and cleared his throat. "Thanks for doing this; it was nice to be able to talk for a minute." He gave us some ideas about where to camp that night, and we were off.

I had thought we were just going for a long walk, which is an adventure in itself. Apparently though, my human had some sort of agenda. The object seemed to be to talk to lots of people, ask them questions and listen to their answers. My green-eyed lady wanted to know how they felt about things; she said she wanted to hear the truth from real people, so she listened to their stories. When we got to the next town, she listened to more stories--and told the new people the stories she had heard in the previous towns. And so it went, from the Mendocino Coast of California, to Keyenta, Arizona.

As we walked, we got more attention. Throughout northern California, newspapers wrote articles and press releases were sent out to tell of our impending arrival. At each town we went to the library because "librarians know everything," and we went to the newspapers in the towns that were large enough to have them. We arrived in Sacramento on day sixteen. My lady went up to the front desk and asked for the editor, as she did everywhere else. The clerk called upstairs and moments later a man came trotting down the stairs. He seemed excited.

"I'm so glad you stopped by our office; I was hoping you would! I got the press release this morning. Do you have a place to stay? Do you have plans this evening? Oh, have I got a surprise for you!" He was really excited.

Once we set up the tent on the deck of some of this man's friends, a couple of nice young students, we were off to the college auditorium. There were places where my lady would go in and leave me at the door to guard the backpack, but she just brought me into most places and people didn't question it. Maybe it was because I was so well behaved.

I lay down at her feet in the auditorium. There were many people there, and I sensed a great deal of positive, respectful energy for the man who was speaking--the man they referred to as a doctor. There were a few people on stage, actually, sitting at a long table. One man seemed to be in charge, and he would let the audience ask questions then he would let the people sitting at the long table answer them.

I did not understand a lot of the words, but I got the idea of what was happening. Apparently, this doctor exposed someone for lying, with something called the "Pentagon Papers." As my lady sat there listening, a man came up to her and shoved a microphone into her hands. She stammered, shook her head and tried to push it away. She looked to the editor who smiled and shrugged.

"This is good. You want some attention, right?" he encouraged.

When she was called on, my lady with the green eyes stood up; her hands were shaking as she read the letter she had written to a woman she referred to as "the first lady." This letter explained that she was walking and talking to people so she could learn, and so she could bring the people's true feelings to this first lady. Then she plopped back down in her seat, forgetting to ask anything. Her face turned an even deeper shade of reddish purple when some people turned around and gave her dirty looks, as though she was wasting everyone's time.

The man in charge said, "Well, since that wasn't a question, let's move on."

Then the doctor spoke up, "Actually, I would like to address what this woman has said." And with that he rescued her. He addressed her issues and encouraged her to continue in her pilgrimage. He was a strong man with a gentle voice; I could feel her relax as she listened to his words. When the event was over, people started to come up to my lady. They smiled and shook her hand and gave her money to help us keep going.

"Some of them didn't understand. But you got your message out there, obviously," said the editor as another person handed her twenty dollars and hugged her.

We walked up to the front of the auditorium to meet the nice doctor from the stage. When it was her turn my lady approached the table.

"I just wanted to shake your hand; it's so good to meet you. And thank you for the save back there; I had no idea they were going to hand me a mic."

And that was almost the end of it. But as they were shaking hands, she looked down at the table to see a paper coffee cup with a green picture of a woman on it, in front of this famous activist.

"You're drinking *their* coffee," she accused with a grin and a raised eyebrow.

"I didn't buy it! Someone gave it to me when I got to the stage; I haven't even taken a sip," he protested. The people around us chuckled as we moved along the line.

There were several articles written about our walk. However, the article in the Sacramento paper was her favorite; she said it tickled her when she saw both of their names in the same story, and I thought they took a nice picture of us. The photographer took us out to the road on which we would continue. He had my lady put on her pack and kneel down next to me. That was all well and good until it was time to get up. Her legs still weren't quite strong enough to lift herself while wearing the backpack.

"Um ... could you help me?" She laughed as she held out her hand.

The following morning we were heading toward South Lake Tahoe. Our young hosts had made peanut butter and jelly sandwiches for us to take and wished us well.

My lady and I had an agreement between us: I protected her from dangerous humans, and she protected me from dogs that looked tougher than me. Passing by a driveway, we heard a throaty warning-growl, which became barking and then attack-mode-snarling. And this sound was getting closer. We both saw him at the same time, neither of us panicked--after all he was hooked to a pretty sturdy-looking chain. My lady was grinning, I think at the thought that in a second or two the charging dog would be out of chain, and we were both anticipating the inevitable "yipe." However, the joke was on us. He kept coming! One end of the chain was indeed attached to the dog; however, the other end was merely dragging behind him, and he was moving at an alarming rate. I tried to puff up and look big.

The next thing I knew, my human had pulled me behind her and was holding me close and tight. She pointed her finger at the dog and yelled, "NO!"

Okay, you could have knocked me over with that proverbial feather that humans speak of. The dog stopped. He just stopped right there in his tracks and looked at her.

"You go home!" She bellowed and pointed toward the house. I think he was as shocked as I was because he just stood there looking back and forth between the two of us. So she repeated the order, adding, "NOW!" And he turned around and sulked back to his house.

When he was out of ear shot she let out a deep breath and looked down at me, "I can't believe that worked." She looked up at the sky and said, "Thank you," then she started laughing. *Laughing!* While she stood there being ridiculous, I emptied my bowels.

On day twenty, we arrived in a town called Placerville, I waited with the pack while my lady went into the newspaper office. When she came out, she said that a woman was going to pick us up and give us a place to stay for a day or two. As much as I like walking, I was excited to rest and play for a bit. My lady needed the rest, too. As we walked through Folsom she had twisted her ankle as we were climbing a hill to get to a secluded spot to sleep, and had been limping ever since.

A tall, graceful, gray-haired woman drove up a few minutes later. She introduced herself and took us to a large house were several people were staying.

While there, we learned of another lady, called the Peace Pilgrim, who walked a *lot* farther than we ever did. As we entered the house, in the corner, stood a blue smock and a pair of flat blue sneakers on display. There were pictures, and movies about this beautiful woman on a pilgrimage of over 25,000 miles talking about peace. I was just surprised by the fact that she was walking alone, that there was no canine at her side. How did she stay safe? And who did she talk to as she walked?

I wanted to stay here; it felt safe. It was calm, nothing hurt my senses--no harsh noises or smells--and everyone seemed more relaxed than the people we encountered in town. And there was music. The gentle, gray-haired woman played the guitar and sang each morning. Such tranquil melodies floated from this lady. Right before I fell asleep, as I lay at her feet, I saw that my lady was smiling ... and tears were slipping from her glistening eyes as she listened.

After a few days, we were off again. In South Lake Tahoe we stopped to camp before heading into Nevada. It was a sunny, warm day when we arrived. After talking with some young people in a book store, we were invited to share their campsite. During the night it snowed, turning our tent into an igloo and making it nearly impossible to leave as the snow was up to the middle of my lady's thighs--which meant that, if I stretched my neck, I could barely keep my chin above the snow. So we stayed until the roads were plowed. The campfire, drums and tiki torches made it seem less cold, and a lot of fun, actually. I love the snow! I played with a small puppy, who kept disappearing in the deep fluffy drifts while they all talked and laughed.

Once we got out of California, and down from the Sierra Nevada Mountains, the terrain changed, and we had difficulty walking in the desert.

We had been heading mostly east, on Highway 50, when we arrived in Fallon, Nevada. As she was filling up on supplies, my lady talked to a few people. Through the open door I heard her ask them what was on the road ahead.

"Nothing honey," said a dusty woman who smelled strongly of straw and all kinds of manure. Mmm, I wanted to get closer but I was tied to the backpack.

"There's a whore house about twenty miles down the road, but they won't let you in--men only--unless, of course, you're looking for work," she looked at my lady's feet and slowly lifted her gaze, following the curve of her body until she reached those green eyes, and the right eyebrow that was arched as my lady returned the gaze.

"I own that whore house." She chuckled and paused to collect her groceries. "What you need to do is turn around and go home. It's not safe out there. The coyotes travel in packs and you won't be able to protect her," she nodded to me.

"And honey, there are human predators out there, too. They see a little thing like you, all by yourself, and they will eat you alive."

I was indignant at the comment about her being alone, but I *was* a little concerned about the coyotes. I couldn't see how my hundred-pound human could fight off a pack of hungry dogs, although with all this walking, and toting that pack around, she was getting pretty strong.

My lady had heard a number of naysayers along the way; they said things like, "You shouldn't be out here alone," "Aren't you a little old for this," and "You should be home taking care of your family." We just kept going though. It seemed to me that we should think this through, but I figured she must have a plan. Somehow we always managed each day; many times things were meager, but we always found a place to sleep and some food and water.

She politely thanked the lady for the information and we moved on. We had several more miles to go before we stopped for the day. Once the sun was going down we found a culvert under the highway and climbed in for the night. On one side of the corregated tunnel we watched the sun set. The next morning the rising sun shone through the other end to wake us up. It was actually comfortable and cozy after she put down some padding, and we slept quite well, only ever hearing the coyotes off in the distance.

A few miles down the road we approached a ranch. Oooh! I could smell the manure, just like on that lady yesterday, all *kinds* of manure! *Oh, can we stop? Please? Please, can we stop?* I started whining. I couldn't help it. I was so excited! She looked at me.

"What is your problem, they're all in pens ya big wuss," she chided. She had *no* idea.

As we got closer a man drove his car up to the gate and my lady asked if she could fill her small water bottles.

He rolled his eyes and shook his head; then he said, "Hang on ... I'll drive 'round and pick you up."

Yes! We're going in! Driving up to the house we passed goats and llamas, chickens and cows, horses ... and *donkeys!* Donkeys make the best poop! I was already planning my incursion into their pen as we got out of the car. The woman from the store came out the front door; she was shaking her head.

"What did I tell you," she asked sternly. "You're looking pretty overheated; come on in and we'll get you cooled off. And you can let the dog run; she's not getting out and all the animals are used to dogs."

"Yeah, but Ebony's not used to all these animals. I have no idea how she'll act," my lady said as she hesitated.

"One way to find out, huh?"

Untethered, I played it cool, staying near her and sniffing the ground as nonchalantly as I could muster. My lady is great; she's smart and witty, but since the car accident that she was in a long time before I was born, she can't really focus on more than one thing at a time. So, as soon as they began to talk, I made my move. Darting quickly under the wooden fence and into the donkey pen, I saw it. And it was still *steaming*! I grabbed it and was heading back under the fence when she saw me and squealed. Everything was under control until she squealed--which startled the donkey, which made him start dancing around like he was on hot pavement. He missed stomping on my head by inches, as I dodged the hooves. He did, however, manage to knock me a few feet off course when he whacked me with his right front knee. Again she squealed as I instantly regained my balance and scooted out unscathed. And then she told me to *drop* it.

Again, "Drop it, Ebby! That's gross!"

I did it. I dropped it. And then I lay next to it, lest anybody try to take it.

"Good girl," my lady said as she went inside the house. *Wait for it ...* My jaws clamped down around the manure morsel as soon the door clicked shut. Oh, *baby!* As much as I was enjoying it, though, I only ate half--and buried the other half in case we ran out of food again. She'll be grateful for it when we have nothing.

The room we were to sleep in was a menagerie of feathers, beads, hats, perfumes, make-up, flowery dresses and shoes. She grabbed a boa and draped it over her shoulders, put one hand behind her head and one on her hip, and started wiggling her body.

"Come up and see me sometime," she giggled. I haven't a clue why this was amusing to her, but she was happy, so I was happy.

Later that evening, my lady sat down at the dinner table with the madame and her husband. The man lectured her, for over an hour, on why she should turn around and go home. He gave her all sorts of reasons, even suggested she was not being a good mother. I thought she might lash out at him at this point, but she held fast and quiet. The next morning the manure-smelling woman marvelled at how my lady held her tongue.

"It must've been bleeding pretty bad by the end of the evening!"

When he realized she was not backing down, the woman's husband got out the map and helped my human plan a more suitable route. And, as the next day was called Easter Sunday, we were invited to stay and eat large amounts of food with them. During that time, as my lady helped clean stalls and buck hay, the women talked. At first the other woman kept telling my headstrong human that she was being silly and that "our government can be trusted."

Then, as they sat enjoying dinner the next evening--and not dropping nearly enough scraps for me, I might add--the woman's energy changed. When her husband excused himself to finish some more outside chores, she leaned over toward my lady. I could sense the weight of what she was about to say. I didn't understand it, but I knew it was important, to her anyway.

"I was workin' the bar at my place down the road on September 11. Young private came in and sat down. I knew him and his dad. Honey, he was white as a sheet and his hands were shaking real bad. Poured him a shot of what he likes and asked him what was wrong."

"'I just talked to my dad.' He took his shot and just sat there. When I thought that was all he was gonna say, he says, 'My dad is the one that gave the order to shoot down the plane in Pennsylvania.'"

"Really," my human mused.

During this trek, a lot of people have told her a lot of things. Some were being funny, some were trying to scare her, some were sharing horrific truths and fears; and some were surely just trying to see how much they could get her to believe. She responded to all of them with the same concerned interest and wrote everything down to sort it all out later.

****

CHAPTER THREE

$\mathcal{W}$ith a new course set, we headed south; day thirty-three of our walkabout was a beautiful day. It was going to get hot, but we walked early in the morning to avoid the worst of the heat; sometimes we started as early as 3:00 a.m. On this day, however, we wound up being stuck out in the sun with no shade in sight. We'd walked a little over ten miles. There were plenty of cows and horses roaming in and out of corrals. It was very flat and dry with lots of sandy dirt and tumbleweed which, by the way, are very unnerving when they're coming at you and you're only two feet tall. I barked and it wouldn't stop; I growled--no effect. It just kept coming at me. So I did what any intelligent dog would do. I hid behind my lady's legs.

There was nowhere to put up the tent, nowhere to go. Late in the afternoon, we were exhausted and the only things we did see for shelter were abandoned houses. We had passed several of them. She looked at me then back at one of them. Then she looked around to see if any cars were coming or if any neighbors were in their fields.

"Come on!"

We scooted under the barbed wire fence and high-tailed it into the house leaving a dust cloud in our wake. Once inside, after she caught her breath, she dropped the backpack to the floor and looked around. I didn't like this, not at all. The windows were all gone, pink stuffing hung from the ceilings, and there was trash everywhere. Clearly we weren't the first intruders. My lady picked a room and cleared it of rubble. She sat down on her pack and let out a huge sigh. She smiled as she closed her eyes and rested her head back against the wall for a moment of ...

"AH!" She screamed.

I jumped. *What?*

In the window, less than a foot from where she sat, appeared a huge horse's head! He shook his mane and snorted as we scrambled to the opposite side of the room. I don't know how I missed his approach; guess I was pretty tired, and I was paying attention to the noises coming from the attic.

"Holy shit," she sighed, and slumped against the wall and stared at the horse, who by this time had finished investigating and was backing away from the window to chew on a tuft of yellow grass. As darkness approached, the attic noises got louder. A large raptor was walking around up there, and it was making no effort to be quiet. When we had done the initial scouting of the rooms we noticed a large hole in the ceiling in the bathroom; it was right over the tub, and coating the tub was the largest bird poop I had ever seen. Bird poop, by the way, is *not* good to eat.

"Okay. So this is pretty scary," she looked at me; then she looked around the room as if she thought there might be a solution written on one of the walls.

Suddenly, she hopped up and stated, "I'm putting up the tent!" She set it up in the little room. It seemed silly at first, but I was very happy it was around us when the night sounds began. She zipped us in and we snuggled in our beds as we listened to the cows; they were either being slaughtered, or they were having sex. There was no smell of death the next morning, so I assume it was the latter.

After a few miles of walking the next morning, my lady stuck her thumb out to get a ride. With towns so few and far between, desert walking just didn't make sense. And, we needed to get out of the heat. A man in a large white pick up truck pulled over. My human hesitated when she saw his ID attached to his visor; it told her that he was with something called "Special Forces" in Georgia. She looked at me and I gave no indication that this was a bad idea; I don't know what "Special Forces" meant, but I didn't sense any danger. And it was so cool in his truck. We stayed in his air-conditioned vehicle for five hours, during which time she good-naturedly argued with the man. They spoke of a "School of the Assassins" and faraway places whose names I cannot recall. There was a point when they spoke of a place called El Salvador and her feelings got more intense. Her breathing became slightly shallower, and the words came faster as she spoke of what she saw and learned when she was there for ten days, a few years ago. That was before we met. Luna must have been so happy to get her home safe and sound.

The man's destination was Las Vegas, so that's where we got out. Being stuck at night in a city is very different from being in the country, or even the suburbs. There was nowhere to go, there was nowhere to hitchhike so we could get out quickly, and there would be no guerilla camping.

We walked for what seemed like hours and were still in the city. At dusk, I watched the pack and my lady went into a church to ask where we could stay for the night. When she came out we went to the park across the street and sat in the grass, against a three foot stone wall; we ate some trail mix and jerky and watched kids play on the swings.

"Okay Ebby, the lady inside said they would help me as soon as they are done with their meeting, so we're supposed to wait here." We never saw them come out and no one came over to help.

At one point two police officers approached to talk to us. They looked pretty serious, until they got close.

"Oh, you're not who we thought you were," one of them said. As they started to walk away, my lady told them that we were kind of stranded and asked if it was okay if we slept here. They both smiled and said that would be fine.

"That was weird," she grimaced. "Why were they so nice?"

We both understood why they had smiled, at about two in the morning. That's when the water sprinklers came on. We were lying there, sleeping comfortably, I on my blanket and she in her sleeping bag. One of the sprinklers was directly under her rump, and that's the one that woke her as it popped up and began spitting. It had her on her feet in a split second. She kicked off the bag, grabbed it and the pack and threw them over the wall. Then she did the same to me! I landed on my feet and got out of the way just in time for her to come flying over.

There we sat, soaked through at two in the morning in the middle of Las Vegas. We needed to move to stay warm, so we walked. As we walked, she sloshed.

"Shut up," was all she said when I glanced up at her.

Everything was open, but there was nowhere to change clothes, unless she left me alone and went deep into one of the large casinos. I was very grateful that she didn't want to do that; neither of us felt safe here, and we did not want to be separated. By sunrise the sloshing had stopped and we were getting to the south end of town where we could start hitchhiking. As we passed a hotel, there was a man trimming the bushes by the sidewalk. We stopped to say hello and so that he could scratch my back. Suddenly, there was a noise—fftt, ffft, ffft. And then there were globs of yellow paint appearing on the ground all around us. Fortunately, the kids involved in this paintball drive-by weren't very good shots.

The man moved away from us, laughing, "Somebody's shooting you with a paintball gun!"

"Wow, this place sucks," my lady grumbled as we kept walking. She had her thumb out as we walked and a man in a pick-up pulled over just ahead of us. He was nice and brought us down to Lake Mead and paid for us to have a campsite for the night.

It was beautiful and quiet. The lady that ran the campground asked some friendly questions after we'd paid. When my lady was done washing her socks and hair at the spigot and was about to eat the ramen noodles that had been soaking in cold water for the last half hour, the woman came back with some hot soup and dog bisquits and wished us a safe journey.

In Arizona, we'd walk for a few hours in the early morning then hitchhike to the next town, where she could get more stories and find a place to shower and sleep. We arrived in Flaggstaff for an Earth Day celebration and walked over to a park where people were gathered listening to music, eating and talking excitedly. I could feel my lady relax as she sat on the grass and watched people.

The man that was in charge of the event brought us back to his home where we stayed for over a week as we waited for mail to be delivered. Someone following my lady's blogs online had given me a sweater, for which I was grateful, but I was embarrassed to wear when it there were other dogs around. The sweater and a few other things were being sent to the post office here, so we needed to wait. It was relaxing and peaceful for my lady. I was less relaxed however. Two men lived there, along with two dogs. The dogs were not very welcoming; they wouldn't even let me in the house. The men told my lady that she could use the extra bedroom but that I would have to sleep outside.

"Thank you for the offer, but I can't sleep inside on a bed while she's out in the dirt," she laughed. "It'd really bug me and I wouldn't be able to sleep." So she pitched the tent in their backyard.

In Cameron, on day forty-five, after talking with a group of women at the library we camped in an RV park. The wind was intense! My lady tried, repeatedly, to set up the tent but the wind kept pulling it from her hands. So as I sat under a small tree, she grabbed the backpack and stuffed it inside the tent to anchor it; then she grabbed some large rocks and placed them inside, in the four corners to hold them in place while she attempted to stake it down. In this area the ground was very hard and dry and after a few tries she plopped down next to me holding two bent tent stakes.

"Okay, so we don't stake it down," she panted.

We encountered the first person who intended us harm in Tuba City. All this time, with all the walking in the dark and taking rides with strangers, no one hurt my lady or even threatened her.

There were the teenagers partying up the American River from us as we slept under the stars a couple of weeks earlier. My lady had said we were forgoing the tent because the sky was so beautiful. We were sound asleep, the kids were noisy and we tuned them out as we drifted off. I didn't hear them approaching and was unable to warn my lady. Suddenly, there was a weight laying on us, the stars were gone, and all I could smell was human urine, alcohol and earth.

"No," she screamed. But I couldn't get to her as I was being weighed down and couldn't see; I was completely disoriented. She recovered faster than I did. Just as suddenly as it came, the weight was gone, and I could smell the fresh air again. She was on her feet, yelling at the drunken kids. I could now see that they had thrown a beer-and-urine-soaked blanket over us. We were fine and not in any real danger. Yet we had no phone, no weapon, no pepper spray, just the two of us to protect each other. We were both instantly aware of just how vulnerable we were.

On this occasion in Tuba City, however, we were in a little danger. We were sitting in the shade behind a grocery store, and she was reading the map. A man approached and asked for some spare change. Considering our situation, this was pretty funny. We had no time to enjoy the irony because he spoke again.

"Hey, you're that bitch that's walking around talking to people," he accused and stepped a bit closer. I stood and also moved in closer to my lady. I could sense her fear as she stood and responded.

"Yeah, I am. Did you want to talk about something?" She was still smiling, but I could hear the tremor in her voice. She glanced around in case she needed assistance, but we were very much alone.

"We don't want you around here," he paused and leaned closer, as did I. "You need to leave. What can I do to make you stop?"

"Nothing." The tremor was gone. Anger fortified her as she repositioned her feet slightly to brace for whatever was coming.

I *knew* what was coming; I saw it in his bleary eyes. He pulled back his right fist. The hair on my shoulders stood up. I bared my teeth as he shoved his fist forward, hitting her on the left side of her chest, just above her heart. I lunged at him as she fell back into the concrete wall, hitting her head hard and slumping to the ground. My leash was attached to the pack and stopped me short. My jaws snapped shut on air as my whiskers grazed his chin.

Trying to get away from me, the man fell back, tripping on the curb, and just sat and stared for a moment as I continued to snarl at him, standing between him and my human; the pack held me fast and my snapping jaws were inches from his face. He backed away and stood, grumbling drunken threats, then staggered down the path. As my lady's eyes re-gained their focus, she pulled me close and hugged me as she rubbed the bloody lump on her head.

The day before, we had learned that the president's wife was going to be in Keyenta talking about education. My human was very excited. We got a ride the rest of the way and started walking through the town. As we did, she talked to people on the way. She wanted to know where this first lady would be, if she could get near, where the press would be, and so on.

It was late in the afternoon, we had not yet eaten, it was very hot, and *some*body was getting cranky. We approached a church as my human said that they should be able to give us some water and food, and maybe an idea about where to stay for the night. The priest came to the door when she rang the bell. He told us that he could not let us into the church, but he would heat up a can of soup we could eat out here on the steps.

As she took the chicken soup, my lady asked the priest what was going on here. She told him that people wouldn't talk to her and she that was actually threatened. He explained that she wasn't welcome here. When she asked why, he was pretty direct.

"Because you're white and because they don't want anybody making trouble while the first lady is here, especially an outsider."

"Seriously," she balked, "you're white. And what do they think I'm going to do, anyway?" When he just stared back at her, she took a deep breath and tried again, "Okay. Can you tell me where I can camp for the night?"

"You can't camp here. Many of their ancestors have been buried here; if you pitch a tent outside you could be desecrating a gravesite. People do not sleep on the ground here; it's disrespectful." This was one of those times when she wasn't sure what to believe. It didn't matter though. We weren't welcome.

After finishing the lukewarm soup, she left the bowl and spoon on the side of the steps, as the priest had long since closed the door on us. As we were walking down the driveway, two Reservation Police cars blocked our exit, lights flashing. The men in brown shirts got out of their vehicles, hands resting on their belts.

"You got some ID," one man asked.

"Have I done something wrong," she challenged as she handed him her license. I let out a small whimper. She was hot, tired and frustrated. And now she was getting angry.

"We've got a report that you're walking around asking questions about the first lady."

"So?"

"That's raised some concerns. Given the circumstances, you are deemed a national security risk. We must insist that you leave town immediately; otherwise, we will place you in jail." He recited lines he must have memorized earlier.

"You're kidding, right?"

"No ma'am, we are not."

"I haven't done anything wrong! I have been walking all day. No one in this town will tell me where I can camp or give me any directions. The people here are so rude. And some guy actually slammed me into a wall back there," she pointed in the direction of Tuba City, "I mean, what the fuck did *I* do? And now *you're* going to threaten me? Since when are we not allowed to go where we want in this country?" It seemed to me a bad idea to yell at this man, but he actually took a step back, so intense was her fury.

"'Ma'am," he smiled an unfriendly smile, "you are not in the United States. This is the Navajo Nation. Just find a way out of town or we will give you a place to stay tonight," he threatened politely as he handed her license back. Then they got back in their vehicles and drove away; the dust from their tires made me sneeze.

My lady's legs seemed to give way and she just kind of crumbled. Some dust poofed out around her as she hit the ground. And there she sat, just staring ahead. A few quiet tears left tracks in the dust on her face.

"Okay, Spirit. I'm so tired, and I don't know what to do anymore. I thought this was what I was supposed to be doing," she cried to the sky. "Please bring me clarity." She took a deep breath and let it out slowly.

"Okay. I've been worrying about my son. He says everything's fine when we talk on the phone, but my gut says different. I can't stay here. I've never been in jail, and I don't want the first time to be in another fucking nation. Oh man, the women in there would *hurt* me! If I go forward, I go deeper into the Navajo Nation, where they don't want me and where we will be alone. I could hitch out, but it doesn't feel good. We would still be in the middle of nowhere in a stranger's car, at night ... Oh, Ebby, what should we do?"

We sat there for awhile as she waited for clarity.

"We need to go home," she stated after sitting silently in the dust for almost an hour. With that, she struggled to her feet, brushed off the dust, hoisted the pack and we trudged back the way we came. And just like that, we were going home.

It was dark when we got back to Tuba City. After that were miles of desolation--not a good idea to head into that in the dark. In the morning there would be tourists and people commuting to the next town. So my lady found a place to hide in the tent. There weren't many options, but she felt she wouldn't be desecrating any burial places if we camped behind one of the closed roadside stands.

We ate energy bars and drank the last of the water, then we spent a restless night, each of us barely sleeping; there were a lot of disturbing noises from the road and from the desert. Just before dawn a truck pulled up and the door opened and shut. As we looked through the flap, a man peeked around the stand and saw our tent, then he finished peeing and left.

It took two rides to get back to California. The first from a lady on her way to work. The next, from a trucker with whom we rode for twelve hours; he got us to a truck stop in southern California.

"Well, there's enough room for us in the bed, but the dog has to sleep on the floor," he leered at my lady. He had been regaling her with tales of his sexual encounters during most of the the trip. She just smiled and nodded as this toothless man continued with his stories.

"Yeah, no. Ebby and I will sleep under your truck," she countered. "Thank you for getting us here; we'll see you in the morning."

After another exhausting day, we reached the last stretch before going over the hill back to the coast. As we walked along Highway 20, having just been dropped at an exit from Interstate 5, my lady finally began to notice the clouds heading for us. I had felt the storm approaching for some time now, but she didn't notice it until we were a mile from any shelter. She refused to turn back, though. It was just a mile back to the last gas station, and we could have made it. But she just would not turn around. I could sense her increasing desperation to get home. The closer we got, the more intense her anxiety. She tried to get a ride, but no one would stop. Suddenly, we were being pelted with white balls of ice. And they hurt! She grabbed the poncho and pulled it over her head. Then she grabbed me, sat on the pack and pulled me in under the poncho to shield me from the ice.

Once the storm slowed, it was dark. My lady put up our tent right on the side of the road. Cars were passing within feet of us. I could hear the water splash and hit the tent as they passed. This felt very dangerous, the slightest deviation could have any of these cars slipping on the ice and plowing right over us in the dark. But there was nowhere else to go. So we climbed in and she dried us off the best she could. There was very little sleep that night for either of us; she mostly just sat holding me close to her as she shook, although it was not cold at all.

The next day, day fifty-one, as we turned onto Highway 1 heading north to our house, we passed the man that smells bad. He was on my lady's bicycle, heading south. She saw him, but said nothing, although I could feel her body tense. When we entered the house, her face fell. It was pretty messy, and it felt cold and damp. The first thing she wanted to do was to take a shower; however the tub was filled with dirty water and the drain was clogged. The refrigerator was empty and the sink was full of dishes; piles of dirty laundry were strewn throughout the house.

"Oh my god," she sighed, "What is *wrong* with him? I wonder how long it's been like this. Oh, Sweetie, I'm so sorry." She looked at her son's picture on the wall as she spoke.

While we were away, the man did not do as she had hoped; she cried that he did not even pay the rent--even though he had been given the money to do so. Along with many other misfortunes, the man had abandoned my lady's little pick-up truck on the side of the road about twenty miles away. It had broken down and he'd just left it and never gone back. When she went to retrieve it, the front seats, the battery and the stereo were all gone, and the windshield was smashed in. I know she liked her little truck very much as she had bought and paid for it by herself, and could feel her sadness when we saw its condition.

Later, when she asked her son why he didn't tell her about any of this when they talked on the phone, he told her that the man stood next to him when they talked so that he couldn't say anything. At that moment she said she realized that they should have had an emergency word, something he could casually say, so that she would know he was in danger and she could return immediately. However, she had trusted this man that smelled so bad, and it just hadn't ocurred to her.

After cleaning up the best she could, we went back out to the street. We got a ride fairly quickly and headed straight for her son's school. The classrooms each had their own doors to the outside so we walked right up to his room and stood in the doorway. We couldn't see him until another little boy spoke out his name to get his attention. The teacher shooshed him then turned and saw us.

"It's your mom," he whispered loudly, as kids do.

The whole class turned to see us in the doorway; and there he was. Mother and son's eyes met and neither could speak. The blue-eyed boy slowly rose from his seat and made his way quicker and quicker to his mom. And there they stood in the doorway, hugging tightly and crying. After a moment, applause rose from the children and the teacher, who was crying unabashedly.

****

Chapter Four

$\mathcal{A}$fter reuniting with our boy, we had all gone into the Village of Mendocino to see some friends and look for my lady's husband. As we stood talking to a few people out in front of the red-painted health food store that looked like a church, the man that smelled bad rounded the corner of the savings bank, and crossed the street when he saw us. She walked into his arms as their friends stood by. I was right at her side as she stiffened and tried to pull away from him. We could both smell the sour stench of alcohol that permeated his entire being. But he tightened his grip and continued to smile as he whispered that she shouldn't ruin this moment.

I could feel her distress; I didn't know what she was thinking, but I sure was able to sense her feelings. I felt surprise, betrayal, worry, and then outrage. Yet, to a casual onlooker she was just happy to see him.

That evening, her son asked if he could stay overnight with his friend. As much as he had missed his mom, I could feel his need to be away from the house. The man had been drinking a lot, and I saw him swallowing some white pills. After he yelled at and threatened a man in a suit and tie who had unwittingly knocked on the front door, he went after my lady. He grabbed her hair and slapped her. I rose and began barking. This time I felt her fear, and this time I saw her fight as he pushed her to the floor. Before I knew what was happening, he turned and came at me; he grabbed my collar and pulled me into her son's room and shut me inside. I could see the lower part of the scene from under the door as I scratched to get out. She had gotten pretty strong, but she was still so little compared to him as he tied her, face down, to the coffee table. I could see her hands turning purple as she struggled to free herself, and I could see his bare legs come from behind. Then she screamed.

When my lady with the bright green eyes decides something, that's it. There can be a discussion, but her mind will not be changed. She says she is listening to her gut, or her "voice." As silly as her methods seemed to some, she would not be deterred when she felt strongly. Being a dog, I agree with her way of thinking wholeheartedly as most all of my decisions are based on instinct, and my life is pretty good.

She said she felt very strongly that she needed to continue traveling and talking to people, but she also refused to be separated from her son again. So after procuring a van to carry all of us and getting the lessons they would need to work on as we traveled, she took her son out of school and we were off to Colorado. The man who owned the coffee company in the Noyo Harbor donated the money for my lady to get the van so that we could continue with the trek.

"I'll drive the van but I'm not going to do anything else to help you with this," the man who smelled bad grumbled as she was packing. Later, she said that this was the only promise he ever kept to her. He drove, and that was it. I still don't understand why she let him come along. He didn't feel so much like our pack leader since we returned. Something had happened to my lady as we walked; I sensed a new kind of strength. I felt the beginning of a huge change. She still behaved the same, but she seemed to be playing a role. What was on the surface was not reflecting the tumultuous shift happening inside. I imagine that he felt something too; maybe that's why he attacked her on the night of our return.

She chose to continue from Colorado because it was just past the Navajo Nation where we had stopped. We headed for the Four Corners area and a place called Durango, following the path we originally took. In Flagstaff her husband started drinking again as he attempted to fix the alternator in the van. Halfway through, he got too frustrated and too drunk to continue. He yelled obscenities at her, then walked off, leaving the alternator sitting in the parking lot of the car repair shop.

Grabbing her wallet, she went in to see if someone could help, then she came right back out, grumbling that her wallet was empty. Fortunately, she still had the phone number of the man we had stayed with on Earth Day. He came and put the alternator back in. Then the three of us--my lady, her son and I--stayed at his place for the night. The other man and the dogs had moved out, so I rested comfortably inside.

The following morning we were parked in town, deciding what to do and preparing to continue without him when he showed up. As he explained later, he spent the night in jail because he was "just trying to wash his hands" at the bus station--where he was buying a ticket back to California with the money he'd removed from her wallet earlier that day.

Once we had found a camping spot, we went into Durango and my lady went into a bookstore as we waited in the van. She emerged with a gift for her son. Her husband grumbled that we didn't have money to waste, but her son had been asking for a book about a boy wizard for a while now, and today was his eleventh birthday.

"I am getting this for him. Geez, how can you possibly be such an asshole? And when you start contributing then you can object, k?" She smiled widely with her mouth, but not her eyes. Oh yeah, there was definitely something different.

As my lady sat at a table talking to people outside a health food store, her son sat on a bench and read his book. I looked across the street to see a man with a camera aimed at my boy as he read; he approached my lady and asked if it would be okay if he put one of the pictures in the local paper.

Once she had given permission to the photographer she returned to talking to people. A tall woman with long flaming hair approached the table. Once the woman had written in the book, she invited us to park at her home while we were in Durango. She had a friendly family, and I had fun playing with the children.

One afternoon as my lady was cleaning out the van, we suddenly heard her cry out. Her husband helped her out of the van and she sat down.

"I was leaning over the back seat and I slipped," she cried. She said she had landed on her left side, cracking a rib. For the next couple of days she could not walk or sit, or breathe for that matter, without a great deal of pain.

"We have to keep moving! What am I going to do? How can I walk?"

"If I may make a suggestion," said the woman that took us in. "I have a friend. Now, you may not believe in this stuff, but she's a healer. She may be able to help you."

My lady did not balk and was eager to let her try; although, she did insist that I accompany her into the woman's home. Our hostess had to help my lady walk into the house, such was her pain. I lay in the corner as the women spoke for a few moments.

Her home was filled with crystals of different sizes and colors, some hanging in the windows and reflecting rainbows onto the walls. At least a dozen candles, of varying aromas--vanilla, spices, a hint of citrus--burned throughout the room. Glass figurines of fairies and dragons lined the window sills, brightly colored sarongs hung in doorways and over windows. The combination of candlelight and streams of sunlight that shone through cracks between sarongs, illuminating strips of incense smoke, gave this home a comfortable, soothing, and surreal feeling.

She had my human lie down on a long cushion on the floor and pull up her shirt to expose her ribs. The woman chanted some words I recognized mixed with some I had never heard; she shook drops of oil onto my lady's ribs and lightly touched them with the tip of a large golden feather.

"Okay now, sit up," she gently prodded my lady to rise from her relaxed state on the floor. Very gingerly, expecting the pain I suppose, she rose to her elbows. Her eyes widened slightly. Her hands on the floor, she pushed herself to a sitting position, and one of those priceless looks of surprise and utter confusion came over her face.

The women sat on the couch and talked for the next half hour, and our hostess placed some cards on the table between the two women. At one point she paused. Her face looked both sad and intrigued at the same time. She looked my lady in the eyes.

"Oh, honey, you have to walk alone."

"So that means no other moms are going to walk with me?" Earlier in the trek, my lady had encouraged other moms to join us as we traveled.

"It is up to you to interpret the message; I can only tell you what I glimpse in the cards." She paused and took a sip of tea. "I can tell you that there are angels with you. I can also tell you that I sense that they feel strongly about helping you."

"What does *that* mean?" I didn't know who the angels were but they sounded important.

"It is their desire that you succeed."

It was almost an hour later when we emerged from the house, and my human needed no assistance. When we got into the van, she marveled to her family.

"I am amazed! The pain is gone--really gone. And she didn't even touch me!" She wriggled around to prove her statement. She excitedly told them about the feather and the oil. She mentioned what the woman said about the angels as she chuckled and rolled her eyes with her family, but beneath her joking, I could feel her respect. I noticed she chose not to mention what was said about walking alone as she turned her head and stared past the view from the window. In her reflection I could see the concern and quiet alarm in her eyes.

"Wow Mom, that's cool," her son said. I could feel his impatience, though. He hadn't wanted to come with us and was anxious to return to where we were staying. One of the woman's children was a young girl, about our boy's age. During the several days that we stayed, they spent all their free time together. Before we left Durango, we took the girl with us as we went to a drive-in theater. The kids and I sat on a blanket in front of the van, and we all watched a movie about a lost fish.

Next, we moved on to Salida. The people were nice there and we camped by the Arkansas River. I loved this river; there were so many rocks to collect! As my humans sat on the bank I would wade into the water and start looking for the right rock. When I saw it I would dunk my head under the water and snatch it up; sometimes the water was deeper than it seemed and I'd wind up diving down until just the tip of my tail was sticking out of the water. I'd then bring the rock my humans.

"Oh, that's so sweet; she's giving us a rock," they would coo.

No, I want you to throw it into the water.

Most times we communicated quite well. But there were times, usually when the man was around, when I just could not get my message across. So I'd go back to the river and get another rock and, again, place it at their feet.

"Haha, she's making a rock garden!"

Eyeroll.

On the river there was a coffee shop, and the man there said we could set up a table and talk to people. I liked the place; I could sit on the patio and watch kids playing in the water. Directly across the river, and past the railroad tracks, was a place the local residents called Hollywood. We visited that side of the river when a woman from the radio station offered us the use of her tub one afternoon. Living out there was also a man who travelled around the country protesting wars. He had a bus that had fake, home-made missles on top. He had painted it dark green and it looked like a military vehicle.

When we left the area, we planned to go to Boulder next. This meant heading north on Highway 285. However, when we got to Poncha Springs there was some confusion. Her husband drove on with the van, intending to meet us about ten miles down the road, and we took his lead. As we walked, people stopped to talk to the three of us. They took videos and encouraged us as we climbed the road. We had a good time, my lady and my boy talked and laughed as they walked. I was completely thrilled; it was always best when it was just us. After about eight miles we saw the van parked ahead. The man who smelled bad was looking amused and shaking his head.

As we approached, my lady looked at him and stopped in her tracks. He was leaning against a sign. It said, "50 West."

"Oh no." She looked at her son and then back at the sign, "We've been going the wrong way!" She kind of laughed, as did my boy, but not really. Then, suddenly very tired, we all piled into the van and headed down Monarch Mountain, back to where we had started that day.

"Why didn't you come back and get us when you realized we were going the wrong way," she demanded.

"'Cause, it was funny. Serves you right to have to walk all that way; you should have paid better attention to the signs, I guess," he smirked as he lit a cigarette from the pack she had just bought for him. She said nothing more, just clenched her jaws and stared ahead at the road.

Fairplay was a fun place with lots of open space, and the people were entertaining. As we pulled into town and turned down a few streets, my boy yelled out.

"Look!" He was pointing to a wooden replica of what looked like a piece of poop wearing a red hat with white, fur trim, that hung on the side of a building. "We're in South Park!"

At one store, I stood in the doorway as my green-eyed lady talked to the owner about her walk and asked if the woman had any comments to contribute. A large man approached the counter as the woman was telling my human that she wasn't interested in what she was selling.

"'Scuse me little lady, but I think you should leave," he drawled.

"I'm not selling anything; I just want to know how you feel about a few things." She smiled and turned to look at the man that had spoken as he pushed his long oil-skin coat back to reveal a large gun on his hip. This was one of those moments when my lady was completely speechless; as her mouth hung open, I could feel her sincere and utter bafflement as she backed out of the shop to where I was standing. Laughter exploded from inside the store as she stepped down onto the sidewalk.

"Okay, Ebby, what the fuck?"

As we walked around we noticed more people; we saw women wearing huge frilly dresses and feathered hats. The men all wore cowboy hats and their spurred boots made funny clinking noises as they walked. We sat on a bench outside the library, waiting for her husband and son to return from the gas station. She burst into laughter after noticing a flyer tacked to a pole.

"I'm such a dork! It's a fair!" She continued laughing until she had to wipe her eyes and blow her nose.

There were still problems with the alternator, so my lady spoke with a man who told her to go to the huge hotel in town and ask for the head housekeeper. He said that her husband was a "whiz with engines" and would probably be able to help. Sitting out on the large porch, I watched my lady through the open doors. She approached a woman in the lobby and asked about getting help from her husband.

"I'm kind of busy right now," she snapped, "I've got fourteen rooms to clean and my girl decided not to show up. You'll have to come back later." She turned to walk away.

"I know how to clean rooms," my lady piped up. The woman stopped and spun around.

"For real?"

"Uh-huh, I ..."

She did not get to finish the sentence because the woman had grabbed her arm and began giving her instructions. My human turned back to me and laughed as she was being propelled down the hallway.

"Hang on, Ebby. I'll be back in a little bit."

"Okay, you take the ones on this floor; here's the diagram. I'll go upstairs and get started." Her words faded as she scurried down the hallway with my lady in tow.

We had a perfect camping spot outside of town, with lots of beautiful smelling flowers, and after the past few days of rain there was a multitude of mushrooms to be picked. We parked and got out to stretch our legs, and I sniffed the air. There was less oxygen here than on the coast. But the air was crisper, and fresher somehow.

The man that smelled bad walked over to the bushes to relieve himself as she was unfolding the tent with her son's help. Suddenly, screaming disrupted the peaceful meadow; a stream of profanities burst from the man's bearded face as he emerged from the bushes, cradling his private parts. He hadn't been drinking since we left Flagstaff and although he was grumpy, as long as he wasn't drinking, neither of them was intimidated by him in the least. So once he was able to communicate what had happened, my lady and her son were unable to control their laughter. The tears ran down her face as she spoke to her son while the man dug for a piece of ice from the chest.

"Remember the other day when you were asking me what karma was?"

"Uh-huh," he said.

They both looked at the man and back at eachother.

"Oh, so that was a karmic bee sting," he exclaimed and they both lapsed into a whole new fit of laughter.

After a week in Fairplay, the alternator was bandaged and my lady had worked several days at the hotel so we had some money for food and gas. We got to stay inside the hotel while she worked. The man who smelled bad drank and stayed out in the van while we enjoyed the room. Next stop, Boulder.

When we spoke with a very nice lady in a "peace and justice" center in Boulder, she told us about something called a bio-diesel bus that was travelling around the country; it was to be at the college the following day. Two people would be speaking--a woman who sat for two years in a redwood tree that she had named "Luna" to protect it from being cut down, and a blonde man who I remember seeing on the television as my lady laughed at a show about people that spent so much time in a bar that everyone knew their names.

Later we went to the library. We all waited in the van while she went in to talk to some of the ladies inside. She came out and said she couldn't believe it.

"Oh my goodness, the librarians were afraid to talk to me! The first one I approached actually covered her name tag with her hand! Finally, I got to talk to the head librarian. She told me that they were all nervous now since the Patriot Act. She said that they shred and delete all info, pertaining to who sees what, at the end of each day."

Although there was no drinking, the arguing did not stop. While we were in Boulder she told the man who smelled bad to go home because "once again he was ruining everything."

"Are you intentionally sabotaging my efforts? Seriously, you had us walk eight miles in the wrong direction!" She yelled from inside the van as her son and I played outside.

"You're draining me. And most of the money I make or raise goes to feeding your needs. And, for the record, cigarettes and coffee are not staples!"

He dropped us off near a wooded area where we could put up the tent and get an early start hitchhiking in the morning. My lady planned for us to ride back down to Highway 50 and then east into Kansas to begin walking again. She and her son unloaded our gear and her husband drove off. Once he'd pulled away she slammed her pack to the ground.

"He just drove off with our hot dinner!"

The three of us ate trail mix and they talked for a while. In the morning we headed south, and then east toward Kansas.

After a week of hitching and walking we still hadn't heard from her husband. There was no word at all--and he should have been back home within two days. Frustrated and feeling responsible, she started making calls. Even "border-to-border" searches by the police brought no news of him. So my lady made the decision to begin to search for him by hitching and walking west on the route he would have taken.

Her son told her that his father had offered, during a phone conversation, to fly to Colorado to get him and bring him home. When she spoke with him, he promised that their son would be waiting for her return. So her son flew back to California to stay with his father, her second husband, while she searched for the third.

As we began the search she received an e-mail from a woman in Utah--whose husband was sharing a jail cell with the man who smelled bad. Apparently, my lady's husband had been arrested for backing the van into the car of the town's family physician. I could feel her anger when she found out he had "done it again."

We hitchhiked directly to a small town in Utah. On the way my lady went into a library to see if there were any messages for her. When she came out, she was crying and tightly clutching a piece of paper. She sat on a bench in the park and hugged me for a long time as she sobbed. Then she stood, took a breath and we walked away.

"Let's go, Ebby," she said, tossing the e-mail into the trash. During a conversation on the telephone later that day I heard my lady tell that the letter told her that her son's father had taken custody of our little boy.

Apparently, her husband swore that alcohol was not involved. Yet when she found the impounded van there sat two cases of empty beer bottles hidden under some pillows between the seats. At this point, it would have been better for everyone if she just left, if we just went home and took care of ourselves and tried to get her son back home with us; this is what she kept saying to me.

"I should just leave him in there; it's what he deserves. He has caused us so much trouble--and now my son ..." she stopped, jumped up and ran over to a trash can where she emptied the contents of her stomach.

Something made her stay, however. And something made her raise his bail and get him home safely. As she straightened up the van she angrily grumbled that through the thick visiting room glass he had told her that she was responsible for his being in there and she couldn't abandon him in jail in another state; he said she was the one who dragged him out on this crazy adventure in the first place. He kept swearing that he hadn't been drinking, and for some reason alcohol had not been mentioned in the police report so she couldn't prove it.

"What do I do, Ebby?" She looked at me.

I was thinking that she should ask the sky for clarity since that seemed to work in the past.

"I can't leave him here; I have to get him home. That way he can't say I owe him, or blame me. If I went home without him he'd kill me when he got back."

It took a lot of phone calls to many friends, but finally the owner and editor of the paper, for which she had been writing as we traveled, said he would help. This meant that we would have to come back to Utah with her husband for his court date, so that her friend would not lose his bail money, "because he certainly can not be trusted to get there on his own."

My lady sighed and said that by this time there was no kidding herself into thinking that he might be the person he convinced her he was when they first met. But she refused to leave him sitting in a jail in another state and have that weighing on her conscience along with everything else.

Divorce proceedings were started soon after our return to the coast. Upon arriving we found that we had been evicted from another home. Apparently, the money she had given him to send to pay the rent hadn't made it. So my humans put everything in storage and we were back to living in a vehicle.

He held onto the keys and would not let her have or even drive her van--even one night when her son was sick and asking for her to visit him at his dad's home. She tried to grab the keys from him and he punched her square in the face. Her nose swelled and bled, and her front teeth loosened a bit.

So we had to share the van as we had nowhere else to stay. One day she had walked out of a woman's shelter, telling me that if she stayed there they would insist that I stay in a kennel. As uncomfortable as I knew she was, I was very happy she did not choose that option.

My lady got a full-time job and began hiding money. Soon she was able to purchase another van so we could finally live apart from the man that smelled bad. It really was a nice van--very comfortable, spacious and clean.

While she worked mixing colors at the paint store I would lounge in the van and wait for her. I was having a good time, although I missed her when she worked. After work we'd get some food and go out to the headlands to eat, walk around and watch the sunset over the ocean. Then we'd find a place to park and sleep for the night.

She got a second job at a cafe for two hours each morning, before the full-time job started. The owner gave her the key so she could open the place for him. We would arrive there before opening time, and she'd go in and wash her hair and make herself presentable for her day's work. It all would have been perfect, except for the fact that the man that smelled bad would not leave us in peace. We lived in a small town and even after separating she could not get away from him. So although she was smiling and laughing with people, she reeked of fear and anxiety most of the time.

One night we were asleep in the driveway of one of my lady's friends. I sensed him first, then I looked out the window and saw him standing across the street. I didn't know what to do. I know him so my tail went into autopilot and began to wag. I knew he meant us danger though, so I was growling to warn her. She had just fallen into that deep sleep and only came out of it slightly.

Raising her head, she pulled back the curtain and saw him.

"It's just some guy, Ebby. Go back to sleep." This is maddening sometimes; she knew better. If I growled she should pay attention. But the drowsiness of half sleep won out, and she drifted back off.

He came at the van and I saw something shiny in his hand, gleaming in the streetlight. He appeared to punch the left rear tire then the front one on the same side, then he ran away. I barked louder and she got up, looked around and went back to sleep. Couldn't she hear the hissing of the air escaping the two left tires? Could she not feel the van listing?

The next morning she got up, moved to the front, and started the engine. As she backed up the flat tires thunked.

"What the hell?" She got out and saw what had happened. "Son of a bitch."

She called the police, as there was a restraining order that was supposed to keep him away from us, but no matter how many times she called they always said the same thing.

"Sorry, we can't do anything about this, no one saw him but you. But please don't hesitate to call again if you need assistance." He even caused a scene in the grocery store when he saw her van parked there one day. He went in and stood by the checkout line close to the exit; through the open door I could hear him yell at her.

"You owe me! Give me money and I'll walk away," he bellowed in his drunken stupor. After all that he had stolen, broken and just plain ruined, I know she would have laughed when he said that, but she was too scared. He followed my lady outside and threw a cup of hot coffee at her that soaked the front of her sweater. The police came again; however, this time her son was sitting in the van with me and saw most of the incident. This time they had to make a report because there was a witness. But for some reason he walked around free, as he waited for his day in court.

The weight that my lady had gained back after walking was gone again; she ate one small meal each day and got very little sleep. She made many attempts to achieve calm and clarity. Every morning she listened to spiritual music and chanted before going in to work. However, I sensed no relief. Fading was that smell from when we first met, the comforting one that I don't have a name for, and creeping into its place was one similar to the smell of her, now, ex-husband. It was just a trace, but I sensed that it would get stronger the longer we stayed in this situation.

In the summer of 2006, I had been feeling something was going to happen. One evening we drove to her son's house, where we had been parking for the last week to avoid her ex.

It was a beautiful place a few miles in from the coast, with many trees and a waterfall toward the back of the property; huge black birds chuckled at us from the treetops. Her son's grandfather had aptly named it, "Raven's Fall." We went inside and my lady explained to her son that we had to leave. She didn't tell him earlier because she didn't want to be the cause of him lying to his dad. She also knew that his dad and grandmother would never be able to keep quiet and, somehow, the man that smelled bad would find out and sabotage our escape.

She explained as best she could to our boy and his grandmother that she was always afraid.

"And, I don't want you to be embarrassed by having a homeless mom; Sweetie, no one will rent to me here.

"Besides everything else," she pulled out an envelope and handed it to her former mother-in-law, "I just got this in the mail. It's a subpoena. It says that we have to appear in court to testify about him throwing coffee at me and breaking the restraining order. The assistant district attorney said that, if they could get the other women together--the others that have gotten restraining orders against him in the past--that he could actually go back to prison because he has such a long history. But you know the A.D.A. as well as I do; I have no reason to believe that chucklehead, and there's no way I'm going to let them put him," she nodded to our boy, "on the stand. We would both be in danger if we testified against him and then they just let him go, anyway--which is probably what would happen. Since I'm the victim, if I leave they have to drop it and my son will be safe, right?"

They cried and hugged; he petted and hugged me. Then we got into the van and began to drive away. My lady looked in the rear mirror and saw her son standing there by the mailbox. She stopped, backed up and got out to hug him, tight, one more time before driving off. Her crying did not abate until we had driven for over an hour and were well past Willits.

****

CHAPTER FIVE

*I*t had been a dry, hot drive through Nevada and Utah's deserts but we were almost there. Sometimes I loved riding in the front seat with the window open with so many smells rushing at me all at once. Most times, though, I liked to curl up and let the vibration of the engine lull me to sleep.

It was one of those times when I was sound asleep. All of the sudden, the gentle vibrations turned to a violent shaking accompanied by a rumble and a kind of flapping sound.

"Ebby, what is that," she asked me as she looked in all the mirrors and out all the windows.

"Whoa," she said, "I just saw something go flying from the back of the van!"

She put on the blinker and pulled to the side of the road, right in front of someone's home.

"Holy shit," she exclaimed as she examined the right rear tire. I looked out the window to see her pick up a fairly large piece of black rubber--which had come off of our wheel. I don't know the why of it, but the tire had just been coming apart in chunks.

She pulled the van into the driveway of the house.

"Oh man, Ebby, what do I ask for, help changing a tire, a phone? I don't even know where the spare is." She looked to me for an answer, as she was pretty shaken. She took a breath and walked up to the front of the house and knocked on the wooden entrance.

"Oh, hi. Do you have a man here," was what came out when the woman opened the door.

"Beg your pardon," the woman asked with her hand on her hip.

My lady laughed nervously and apologized, explaining our situation. As it turned out the lady did not have a man on the premises, but she called her father, who came right over. He and his eight-year-old grandson, a mechanic in training, apparently, examined the tire.

"Well young lady, you are in luck," he looked out from under his floppy straw hat and chuckled, "I actually have a few spare tires back there," he pointed to a pile that stood over fifteen feet high, "and I have one to fit your van. So we can get you fixed up in no time at all."

"Really? Oh thank goodness! Oh, I really appreciate this," she said to him, and to me she whispered and giggled.

"He called me 'young lady,'" she nudged me.

We sat in the shade with the lady of the house while her dad and son replaced the tire. When they were done, we all sat on the porch. The boy petted me while my lady drank a cool drink and chatted with them.

She tried to pay the man for his trouble and for the tire, and he just brushed it off saying that she should just pass it on. We heard this several times as we traveled. There are so many kind, generous people out there. My lady always commented on this fact, saying how surprised she had been when we first walked.

"When I sit at home and listen to the television or radio, all they talk about is how much we need to fear and mistrust each other. We hear about school bombings, child abuse, rape, theft and terrorists lurking everywhere; we're convinced that we can trust no one. But when I got out there on the road--walking, vulnerable, or when I went to El Salvador--my faith in people was restored. People are so *nice*! The majority of people that I meet are truly good people, people that wouldn't hurt anyone, people that genuinely want to help others."

Mmm, I could smell the water in the air! And I was starting to smell some familiar aromas, but I couldn't quite place them yet. All that desert driving and now there was water, and green grass and trees. Almost as soon as we crossed into Colorado, the change was drastic. I was thrilled and relieved. I wasn't sure where we were going to wind up at the end of this drive; I was just so happy it wasn't in one of those deserts that we just drove through; I do not like the desert. It's so arid and bland; water is what makes the smells come alive!

When we arrived in Durango, where I finally recognized the smells because we had been here before, the first thing she did was take me to the Animas River. I was so excited I could hardly wait to get out of the van! There were very few other people as it was very early in the morning so she didn't bother with the leash. This was great!

We got closer to the river and could see a man throwing a stick into the water for his dog.

Wait! Was that my stick?

"Ebby, no!"

It was no use; I couldn't stop. I dove into the water. I am a very good swimmer and I passed the other dog with no effort, snatching the stick as it bobbed in the current. The swim back was tricky however, but with only a little choking I was able to out-swim the other dog, while holding the stick and growling to be sure he kept his distance. I could see my lady on the bank, her hand covering her mouth, her head shaking. The man just stood there with his mouth opened; he must have been really impressed with my speed and agility.

Instead of praising me for my success as I emerged from the water, shaking and wriggling with the thrill of the chase, she just said, "Ebby! Shame on you," and took the stick and gave it to the man. He didn't even get in the water!

For two weeks, we walked around town and she talked to people about employment and places to live; she put notes on boards and made phone calls. One morning, she came out of the coffee shop holding a piece of paper.

"K, Ebby, this one's in Pagosa Springs--about an hour away. Some guy is going hunting in the mountains for a month and he needs someone to watch his log cabin. Sounds pretty sweet, huh?"

As soon as we got out of the van, and the man walked out his door to greet us, I knew we should leave. The place was beautiful, and I know it was just what she had envisioned for us--log cabin, lots of trees--except for the man, who had that festering smell.

So we were now in the home of another potentially dangerous person. My lady brought only what was needed, from the van, into our bedroom, making sure that we could leave within ten minutes if we needed to do so. The hair between my shoulders rose slightly every time this new dangerous man came near; he smelled even worse than the man we had just escaped from.

After two weeks of housecleaning and performing chores he rattled off each morning, it became clear that the dangerous man was not leaving. Slowly, I could see the realization of our true situation dawning in her eyes; the following morning, he called my lady out of the bedroom and told her that he was dissatisfied.

"I don't feel I'm getting my money's worth," he said darkly, as she once again refused to let him touch her. He had requested that she put lotion on his back on our first night there, and she politely refused, saying that she absolutely does not like touching people or being touched. Now, he told her that he wanted her to be making him breakfast. He emphasized the last word, paused and looked at her for a moment to let his meaning sink in. I looked at her and could see her face redden slightly. He said, if she wasn't interested in the arrangement, she should think about finding another place to live. Whatever his meaning was, I didn't get it, but apparently she did and boy did it make her angry.

"Excuse me, but I came here to watch your home while you were away. I never agreed to live with you or take care of you. And I certainly did not sign on to be your wife," she said as calmly and politely as possible.

"I'm going to work. You think about it and let me know how you want to proceed," he said as he sauntered out the door.

"I ... ooooh ... his *money's* worth? *Breakfast*? I ... how *dare* he?" It was kind of funny to watch her try to form a sentence; she was *really* angry.

As soon as his truck hit the street my lady went in to action, grabbing bedding, my bowls and her toiletries from the room and tossing them into our van. She was right; it took less than ten minutes. She was still muttering as she was putting his key on the desk by the phone. We both jumped as it rang. After a moment a woman left a message.

"Hi, I'm calling about the caretaking position you have available. I could be there tomorrow to meet with ..."

"Hello?" My lady had grabbed the phone before the woman could disconnect. She explained who she was and what was actually happening here. Through the speaker, I could hear the lady on the other end of the line gush appreciation for the warning.

At the restaurant where she worked, she went in and sat at the bar to talk to her co-worker about sleeping on his couch. He had warned her the previous day, when he found out who she was staying with.

"You should be okay there. But if you see him with a drink, get out immediately," he had laughed, nervously. "You can stay with me until you find a place."

What the bartender neglected to tell her, and what the town's Welcome Lady was all too happy to share the following week as we sat on the patio of a cafe having coffee, was that the man we had been staying with had a police record and a reputation in town. He had been arrested the previous year for what he did to the last woman he lured to his home. She didn't get away as easily as my lady. She visited the emergency room with a battered face, apparently.

"How is this possible?" She was shaking her head and pacing back and forth along the Animas River while I chose rocks from the water and placed them on the bank, hoping to distract her with play. "Oh my god! Why is this happening again? Why do I keep drawing these people to me? What am I supposed to do?"

After checking as many references as possible, then sitting in the van staring at the house for over an hour, we moved into a place about seven miles outside of Pagosa Springs. The man that owned this home was kind and unimposing. He was undergoing cancer treatment, and his health was poor. He had a few extra rooms and was in need of some additional income. We chose a nice little added room with a separate entrance. The smell of his illness made me sad, so I was relieved that we would not be in the main part of the house.

****

CHAPTER SIX

*A*fter almost a year, I could feel that energy again. She was restless; for some reason she was unable to settle in and live comfortably in this town. I could feel her frustration and her need to make a change.

Soon after we moved to Pagosa Springs, she was fired from her job at the restaurant. It was also a bar, and as I sometimes sat on its patio, I watched as my lady repeatedly removed men's hands from her bottom. According to the owner, as he fired her, the problem was that she got so angry--and was so explicit about what she would do to these men's private parts if they touched her a second time.

Having found a more pleasant job at a bakery owned by two ladies, my human made friends with a woman that she worked with. They giggled a *lot* when they were together, and it never took much to set them off. One afternoon I was waiting on the porch of the bakery while my lady and her friend were getting ready to close the shop for the day. There were two owners-- both beautiful, kind, funny women. The woman with the gray hair walked out from the back of the kitchen and said that the ladies needed to rearrange the tables and chairs because they were "having a LIPS meeting in about an hour or so." I could see her put her hands on her hips when she saw both ladies stop what they were doing and look at her questioningly.

"What?"

"Um, LIPS," asked my lady.

"Yes, LIPS. Lesbians In Pagosa Springs," she sighed and rolled her eyes. "Go ahead."

The two women were not able to wait for permission; they were both already besieged by fits of laughter. The owner huffed and walked out the door, petting my head as she passed.

"Honestly, Ebony, they are like little children."

After work on the weekends, we went to a bar that played music. My lady and her friend loved to dance as much as they loved to laugh. I sat in the car sometimes and watched through the window as they danced wildly. Then they would grab their drinks and come out to the patio and smoke cigarettes. They'd reach through the car window and pet me as they talked.

When "I'm not here for your entertainment. You don't really wanna mess with me tonight" wafted out the front door as it opened to let someone in or out, they crushed their cigarettes out and ran back inside to gyrate to the music. When men would pester one of them to dance or "go somewhere," the other would be right there putting her arm around her shoulder saying, "She's with me." As the man walked away dejected, but grinning, they were giggling and clinking glasses.

As much as she laughed and danced though, underneath the smell that I loved, she still had that other smell to her--the festering smell that was still not strong, but was no longer faint.

When we first arrived in Pagosa Springs, I went with my lady to the post office as she mailed off the book of comments that she had collected while we traveled from California to Colorado. A few months later she received a letter from the first lady herself, thanking her for walking and collecting the notes.

"Look Ebby, she even mentions your name in her letter, see," she showed me the letter, and I licked it.

"No!" She wiped it off. "You dork!"

Receiving this letter didn't make her happy though; she sat on her bed and absently scratched my head, saying that she never seemed to finish anything. While we lived there the letter sat in a frame on the nightstand and she looked at it each day, until one day she said, "I gotta try again."

So after a year in this town that "smelled like butt" because of the sulfur in the hot springs, according to her son, we started walking again. We walked about twelve miles the first day. Being out of practice, we were both sore when we limped into the campground. The new backpack had chaffed her side raw and purple bruises appeared across her shoulders and on her hips. The one thing she forgot to pack was a pad to sleep on. Sleeping outside in the mountains, even in the heat of summer, was a new experience for us. It was cold! As we lay there the earth seemed to suck the heat right from our bodies. So she spent the night sitting up and holding me and shivering.

This time felt different; it didn't feel like a fun adventure. It felt like we were running away from something--even more so than when we moved from California. We still talked to people; however, she didn't really seem to care about their responses and she rarely wrote them down. We didn't talk to newspapers, and we walked faster and longer than we should have each day.

When we got to Taos, my lady asked where we could camp and we were directed to a small town nearby, called Arroyo Seco.

As we walked she smiled, "Is this place for real? It's so cute! Everything's adobe--and look, the shops sell their stuff on the sidewalks." Then she looked at the sign above where we were to stay and laughed. "It's a Snow Mansion; okay, let's check it out."

At the front desk sat a young man with green hair; he smiled and greeted us warmly. The place was comfortable and homey; it felt very welcoming. My lady worked in the garden and folded laundry as we stayed in the tent out back; as she worked, she and another lady talked and laughed. This other woman continuously grazed on spinach, kale and other greens from the garden, making her teeth a slightly darker shade of green than that young man's hair.

We were there for a couple of days when one of the other guests asked my lady if she would like to go to the hot springs with him. We had been having meals with him for a few days, and he seemed pretty nice.

"I don't know. Is it expensive," she asked. He shook his head and laughed.

"No need to worry about that; you'll see," he said as we climbed in his jeep, which had no roof. This was a new, exciting experience for me; my senses were being happily assaulted by so many different things rushing by at once.

He drove us around a bit, showing us the area. Then we drove right up to the edge of a cliff and stopped short. I looked at my lady; her mouth was hanging open as she looked at the view of the Rio Grande River in front of us.

"Are you okay?" He chuckled. Her mouth snapped shut and she nodded.

"Oh my goodness ... this is breathtaking," she beamed.

"Hope you're in the mood for a climb," he said as we got out of the vehicle. He pointed down to the river, more than fifty feet below. The sides of the ravine were covered with rocks and boulders.

"Um ..." she hesitated. Her legs were pretty strong but going down hills or stairs always presented a problem for her and caused a lot of pain in her knees, which randomly buckled without notice since that car accident a long time ago.

"Okay, I'm willing to try," she smiled and took a deep breath, then began to follow behind him. It took a while but, slowly--using her arms to support herself between the boulders--she made her way to the water's edge with me following close behind. I took a long drink of the cold, crystal clear water when we got there. She bent over to splash some on her face and as she stood and turned, saw the man removing his shorts and shirt--below which there was nothing but ... man parts.

"Oh," she exclaimed, fingering the pepperspray in the pocket of her cargo shorts. He told her to relax as he slid into the pool of hot water at the side of the river.

"This is it," he explained. "Hop in."

When she realized this was the hot spring he had spoken of, she did relax--a little. There was a natural circle of rocks, in the center of which was a pool of steaming water. She had worn her swim suit under her shorts; as she removed the outer garments and lowered herself into the steaming water, he grinned and rolled his eyes.

"Clearly, you're shy. Hope you don't mind that I'm naked," he attempted to ease her discomfort.

"Nope," she lied. "I'm good. Thanks." She dangled her hand in the cool water of the passing river and I could see her relax as the steaming pool soothed her aching muscles.

We stayed for a few days more, then my lady decided she wanted to do more walking through Colorado. So after getting a few rides we were back in that state, having been dropped off in Pueblo, and walking along Highway 50.

The two of us have met so many interesting people as we've traveled. There was another naked guy, outside of Pueblo; he had pulled over as we walked and asked if we needed help. I could easily smell that this one was a predator. But my lady took him up on his offer. He said we could put the tent in his back yard; then he changed his mind and said we should sleep in the extra bedroom because his neighbors might not like the tent. She elected not to get into the bed or use the shower; she set up our beds in the corner on the floor, by the sliding glass door which opened into the back yard, and made sure the pepper spray was close at hand.

I growled but it took her a while to hear me. It was still light outside, but she had fallen deeply asleep less than an hour after we arrived. When she finally awoke our host had come into the bedroom and was sitting on a bench about a foot away from the end of her sleeping bag, just staring at her as I growled.

When she sat up he said that he wanted her to go out to a bar with him. She opened her mouth to say something then shut it, took a breath and politely declined. She turned back toward the window when he left the room. Just as we were dozing off again, she caught her breath and jumped up.

There, prancing--there's really no other word for it--through the center of the immaculately manicured lawn was our cherubic host. And he was completely naked. As she muttered, "Oh my god oh my god oh my god," she stuffed her bag into the backpack. "Can I not get a break here? They're all the same," she cried.

Then she wiped away a few tears, and grabbed my leash as we scooted out the front door. We ran, or actually hobbled, until we were around the corner and down the road. Odetta Lane was only a couple of blocks from Highway 50, so we didn't have far to go to get back to the main road. We wound up procuring a private little spot in some bushes that night.

The next day we walked from Pueblo to Avondale, then caught a ride to Fowler where a nice man let us stay in a vacant trailer in his RV park toward the end of town. There was a railroad track running by the campground that kept waking us up, but overall, it was very enjoyable. There was no hot water, but my lady took a shower--squealing the entire time--and washed her clothes, anyway.

In a town further east, she spoke with the sheriff when she went into his office to see where it would be safe and legal to camp for the night. He told her we could sleep in the park as there were no events this time of year; he said he'd be sure his officers drove by a couple of times to be sure that we were safe.

We sat at a table in the park for a while, but we were restless. We played ball and we ate, but still we were restless. I knew why *I* was restless--the weather was changing.

"This doesn't feel good. We need to keep moving; let's hitch to the next town." She hoisted the pack onto her back.

It didn't take long to get to Lamar. Once we did, she finally realized that there was a storm coming. So the first thing we did was head for the library and police station, which were located in the same building. When she came out she said that the people inside gave her no help or suggestions. As we stood there, a motorcycle roared up to the curb and then became silent as a man climbed off its back. The brown hair on his head and on his face were both long and cottony, and floated in the breeze as he lumbered up to the door. Under the strong smell of leather, which covered most of his body, I sensed no danger. My lady asked him the same questions she said she had asked inside; he was much more helpful. He wrote on a piece of paper that she had torn from her journal.

"You can stop by or not; if you're comfortable with it, I have an extra bedroom. You'd be safe. Either way, here's my address and phone number." He smiled warmly and walked into the library. She stuffed the paper into her pocket and we headed over to a store; her calves were sore, and I could see the lumps where they were cramping, so she was having trouble walking.

Then we met a lady who kept saying that someone's son was going to save us; I didn't sense any danger, so I really didn't understand. We were in the health food store, asking the clerk where we could camp and this lady approached my human, saying that her boy was away so she could stay in his empty place across the street from her. My choice for shelter would have been man with the leather, but my lady chose to stay with the woman.

When we entered the house, she stopped dead and her mouth dropped open as I growled. The hair was standing up all the way down my back as we stood staring at several large, stuffed, but not yet mounted, elk heads lying on the sofa and floor of the room in which we were to sleep.

"Oh, don't worry about them; they won't bite," she said with a smirk when she saw my lady's face. "Just push them out of the way."

Once the woman was back in her own house across the street, my human scribbled something on a piece of paper and left it on the kitchen counter. We then walked to the corner to look at the signs and get our bearings.

"I wonder how far that guy's house is from ..." she stopped and looked at the street sign.

"No way!" We had driven a few miles from the store to this woman's house, and the man's house was one block from were we were standing. She hobbled down the street to his driveway.

"I love when that happens; thank you, Spirit!"

"Oh, right on." The leather-covered man smiled when he opened the door. He laughed when she told him of our encounter.

"So you feel more comfortable with a hairy biker than a Christian lady," he asked between bouts of laughter.

"A Christian lady with *elk heads*," she added, laughing. "Honestly, you wouldn't believe some of the charactors we've run into. Sometimes it's scary, mostly though, it's pretty funny." She told him about a few of our encounters, including with the prancing naked guy.

"I've just gotta trust my gut; although, when I'm tired or distracted I kind of miss the signals or something," she said, then pointed to me, "so, I rely on her a lot. Although, she never bit my ex-husband, so I don't think that method's fullproof," she laughed.

Even though she had just insulted me, I sat in the hallway outside the bathroom door as she took her shower.

"She growled at me! Wouldn't even let me through to my bedroom," he marveled when my human emerged smelling of soap. She bent down and gave me a squeeze and a kiss on the head.

"*Good girl*," she whispered.

As we sat in the living room after dinner I could feel a drastic change in the air and I couldn't sit still. I felt pressure in my ears and smelled electricity in the air. I walked over and put my head in her lap. She looked up from her notepad and out the front window; the digital clock said it was 6:50 p.m.

"Um ... why is it so dark all of the sudden? And what's that noise?" She had to raise her voice to be heard by the man that sat no more than four feet away.

"I'll turn on the weather channel," he said as he pushed buttons on the remote.

"Whoa," he exclaimed as the noise got even louder. It was a deafening roar, like many large trucks driving within feet of the house. He walked over and opened the wooden front door and we all looked out the screened door. Large raindrops mixed with balls of ice splattered onto the lawn, which now looked like a grassy pond. Then there was the siren which scared me enough that I needed to pee.

"That's the tornado warning," he said as he returned to the computer screen. "We just have to pray." He indicated around his home. "What you see is it. No secret storm cellar or safe room here."

"Hey, this is great. We *were* going to be sleeping in a park tonight. We'll be fine." She walked over to the window; I could see her face in the reflection when the lightening flashed. Her eyes sparkled with the thrill of the storm, then she grinned and laughed.

"Oh man! Can you imagine? We could have been alone in that house with all those heads, no electricity and no information, in this storm. Haha, I would've been freaking out!" She looked at the sky and smiled and her lips moved. There have been many times when she's done that; and I know she was whispering, "Thank you; that could have sucked."

We stayed with him for two nights, during which time my lady rested, wrote in her journal, and talked and laughed with this man. On the second night, we headed over to a truck stop and they had dinner with a friend of his, another biker, while I waited in his truck.

The other man was equally kind and friendly. They sat in the living room talking and laughing far into the night.

At one point, as my lady was in the bathroom, the men whispered together. The friend handed our host something. He, in turn, took something from his leather vest. Then he leaned over and slipped the items into a pocket of my lady's jacket.

We got up two hours before dawn the next morning and headed out. I must have missed something when they were talking the night before, because we were now heading south instead of east. While we walked, my lady was attacked by a swarm of rampant mosquitoes and had to fend off not one, but three growling dogs in the dark. It was pretty scary, actually. We could hear the snarls getting closer and all we could see were their eyes reflecting in her flashlight. We backed down the road, away from their domain, as she kept the flashlight on them, calmly talking to them and telling them that it was okay and that we were just passing by. Thankfully they stopped, in unison, at the edge of the property and stood there growling as we faded into the darkness.

Forty minutes later it started to get lighter ... and she stopped. The look on her face as the situation *dawned* on her was quite hilarious.

"Seriously?" She looked at me, then she looked at the rising sun--which was to our extreme left. "Oh man, I really need to get a compass."

We got conflicting information as she talked to people, but most said that it was not legal to hitchhike in Kansas. Also, there was a great deal of wide open space and she didn't want to get stuck in the middle of nowhere, with no phone reception. So we got a ride through the state with a couple we met while staying at a campsite in Garden City.

After the run-in with the naked guy, my lady turned down several people when they asked if we needed a lift or help, these people seemed to be a refreshing change. It was nice to be assured a ride all the way across the state with this couple. The woman said she was a seventy-three-year-old retired nurse, and she slapped her husband on the shoulder as she bragged that he was eighty-seven years old and had retired from the military. She said they were on their way to a reunion in Missouri.

When we approached a stop sign, the woman startled us by hollering at the man.

"Stop sign! Put your foot on the brake!"

She looked at my lady and explained, "He's going blind, and he's deaf as a door post so I gotta yell." When she saw that the coast was clear she hollered at him to put his foot back on the gas.

"We're gonna die, Ebby," my human whispered to me.

On the second day that sweet old couple drove us into Kansas City. They drove the wrong way down a one way street and pulled into a gas station to fill up, and this was where they left us--over ten miles from Highway 50.

As they pulled away we assessed our surroundings. There was a slight breeze, but instead of fresh air it brought pieces of paper and cups that skittered along the gutters, and the stifling smell of exhaust. The windows were almost all broken in the graffiti laden buildings. Sirens and angry horns blared; as we walked over to the payphone, she said she wanted to see if there was a map, but the book was gone, and the cord to the phone had been cut.

"Okay, this officially sucks." The smell of her fear was almost overpowering; I stood close with my tail between my legs and felt it necessary to snarl at more than one passerby, reassuring her that I was on duty.

She took a deep breath, looked up at the sky and said, "Thank you for keeping us safe."

Then she hoisted the pack, felt for the pepper spray in her pocket, pulled me in close, and began walking. The first man we passed was peeing on a stop sign. She asked the next man for directions and he sent us one way, while the next sent us in a completely different direction. It always seemed to me that she approached the largest, scariest looking men she could find, when asking for directions;

when we'd get close enough I could sense that her instincts were correct, in that the men meant us no harm.

After several blocks of walking, we saw two men talking outside a neon light store. One was a delivery man in a uniform that matched his truck; the other was the proprietor of the store. She approached the delivery man, "because he certainly should know the way out of town" and asked directions. She was surprised when he looked at her, rolled his eyes, and walked away. The other man shook his head at her.

"Oh darlin', you need to come inside my shop." He quickly ushered us inside. "I don't know what your story is, but you really can't be here! You are in the *least* safe part of this fair city."

She explained that we got dumped here but were aiming for Highway 50.

"Get in my truck and I'll drive you out of town," again he shook his head, "this *really* isn't safe. Do you at least have a gun or a knife?"

"I have an Ebby," she smiled weakly and nodded to me, choosing not to tell him of the pepper spray that I could see her gripping in her pocket. I could tell she did not trust this man, but he seemed to be our best option to get to safety.

After my lady had thanked him repeatedly, he dropped us off where it was, once again, green and there were plenty of trees and lawns to be seen. We walked for a few hours, having stopped and talked with several shop keepers along the way, and then she began to stick out her thumb because it was getting late in the day.

A large pick-up truck pulled over. It reminded me of the truck the special forces man drove, the one that dropped us in Las Vegas. It smelled the same, and my lady had the same reaction she did when she entered the other truck. But, as with the last time, I sensed no danger.

My human told him what she was doing when he asked. Then he told her he was a "double distinguished expert" with weapons, and how he worked with seals in something called a covert operation.

She asked about the school in Ft. Benning, and when he said it was classified, she snorted--politely.

I felt her excitement when he told her about the Katy Trail. And she was very thankful when he brought us to a nice safe, clean campsite, right next to an air force base. My lady had smiled and shaken her head when she was surprised to find a couple of twenty-dollar bills in her jacket pocket earlier today as she searched for a tissue, so we were able to afford a site and some supplies. When the sun went down a horn played a song from somewhere, and my lady stood as she listened to it. I was enjoying myself very much; there were flies that had lights on their bottoms, and I was having fun trying, unsuccessfully, to catch them as she laughed at me.

"Wow, cool," she smiled, "I haven't seen fireflies since I was a kid! They were always out on warm nights; some kids made rings out of them but that was so horrible. I didn't even like putting them in jars." She paused and stretched, taking in a deep breath of air.

"Yeah, ya know ... the further east I get, the more childhood memories pop up--thunder storms, ciccadas, lightning bugs--more people, less green stuff, congestion, pollution ..."

An older couple came by the tent to say hello. They said they were the camp hosts and they gave her some papers to look at.

"Ebby, look," she said as she showed me one of the papers they had given her. "This trail goes all the way through Missouri."

The next night we stayed at the fairgrounds located at an entrance to the Katy Trail. It seemed like a blessing that we got to stay there for the night because it cost nothing, and there were showers and everything. Then the stock car races began. They were so loud that my lady had to yell for me to hear her. This lasted way past our bedtime. And then the fireworks started.

Before the races started it was quite nice, though. As we sat resting in the shade, a woman came up to the tent. She said she was from a place called Texas, and I had trouble understanding her words. Fortunately, my lady didn't have a problem.

"'Scuse me; I don't mean to be rude. But are ya'll homeless?" She smiled a big, *very* white smile, "We have some chicken and potatoes if you like." They talked for about twenty minutes after my lady turned down her offer of food--which made no sense to me at all as we were both pretty hungry.

Once my lady told her why we were out here, the woman's tone changed. Where at first she was condescending, she became genuinely interested, and she had her own stories to tell my lady, about flooding in her home state and the fact that people weren't getting the help they needed after some storms.

When we got to the next trailhead, in Clifton City, we had walked fourteen and a half miles. My lady had a pamphlet that told her that there were stores and a camping area; however, we arrived to find a covered bench and a metal outhouse. There wasn't even any water to be had--and we drank the last of our water about a mile before we got there.

"What are we going to do," she asked as she slumped down onto the bench. "Spirit, please help us," she asked of the sky. Her face was very red and she seemed out of breath even though we had been sitting for a few minutes.

My head hurt and I was having trouble breathing, too, as I lay there on the concrete. It took too much effort to hold my dry tongue in my mouth so it just hung out and lay on the cool, shaded pavement.

"Ebby, I'm so worried about you." She was not unaware of my increasing poor health. We were both, however, in the same condition.

Moments later a man coasted down the street on a wobbly bicycle and turned onto the path. He rode over to where we sat and greeted us enthusiastically.

"Do you have any water," was the first thing my lady asked as they shook hands. "The map says there's water here," she shrugged and indicated that there was none to be seen. "She's really dehydrated and I'm pretty worried."

"You look like you could use some water, too. I'll be back in a minute." He took off, back up the street. From the other direction came a young boy on a funny-looking tricycle; it was stretched out so he was almost lying on his back as he peddled. He pulled up and looked at us. He wore a neat shirt that was as white as that Texas-lady's teeth, and shorts with suspenders.

My lady smiled and said hello as I walked over to greet him. He said nothing. She told him that he could pet me, that I was friendly. He said nothing while he petted me. She asked if he lived close by, and he still remained silent.

"Sweetie, I need to ask you a favor." She squatted down so she was at eye level with him. "Could you go back to your house and ask your parents if it would be okay to bring me some water? We've been walking for a long time and there is no water here."

When he just continued to look at her she went on. "I'm afraid she's getting sick," she pointed at me and turned back to look him in the eyes. "Would you mind doing that for us?"

He petted me for another few moments, then turned his trike around and peddled away without saying a word, so I had no way of knowing if he even understood her words.

We sat there resting quietly for a while and the man returned. With a huge smile he handed my lady a bottle of warm, brown water. She smiled and thanked him, but I could feel her distress as she filled my bowl. I was not deterred; it was *water*! It was actually pretty safe; it just tasted like metal. Even after I drank it, she held out. I guess the fact that I drink from oily puddles and eat donkey poop didn't help convince her that my judgement was sound.

They sat and talked for a long time; he was very friendly and talkative. He told her that he hung around the trail head and assisted bicyclists. This was a major thoroughfare for cyclists, apparently. So he would keep tires and chains and other miscellaneous items to repair bikes as they broke down on the trail. As he spoke, I wondered why he didn't repair his own bike.

He stopped mid-sentence when he saw what was coming down the trail. My lady turned and smiled brightly. The young boy had returned, trailed by six of his siblings. The boys all in crisp white shirts and the girls in pretty floral dresses, their hair neatly braided and secured at the backs of their heads with pins and small bonnets. None of them spoke to us; they just whispered and giggled among themselves as they each, in turn, handed us a plastic soda bottle of some of the coldest, clearest, sparklingest water I had ever seen.

"Oh, bless you!" She opened a bottle and grinned with satisfaction as she restrained herself and slowly sipped the ice cold water. Then, as the man was distracted by trying to talk to the children, she dumped out my water and replaced it with what the children had brought. I had to wait to drink it; it was much too cold for me right then.

"Thank you, so much. That was very kind of you, and please tell your parents I said thank you," she said to the boy. The corner of his mouth raised slightly, as if he was going to smile. Then he turned and slowly peddled away with the other children walking behind him.

"Aaallrighty! I have no idea how you got them to do that! They are not permitted to interact with anyone from the outside world. Lots of people come by here; never saw *that* before." The man rubbed his stubbly chin as his gaze followed the giggling children.

This man stayed until almost dark. Before he left he warned us that a storm may be brewing, and they can be "pretty sudden and dangerous in these parts." We had intended to sleep on the bench. He listed some creatures that we may encounter, assuring us that the wildlife was "nothin' to worry about" as long as we left them alone. Even I could tell that this was one of those times when the person was trying to scare her. There was nowhere to stake the tent, as the ground in this clearing was covered with concrete, so we slept on the covered bench. The storm never came and it actually turned out to be a lovely night.

It took much more than the usual twenty minutes for us to get road ready the next morning. We were both very tired, and had no choice but to continue as there was no actual town here that we could see, and we had to find food and more water.

It took over six hours for us to walk the twelve miles to Pilot Grove. Walking was slow; she was still limping on a cramping leg that had not yet healed since Lamar. The pack was so heavy in this heat; my leash was always tight as I pulled her along. Then she fell. People don't think that dog's laugh or that we have a sense of humor, but I assure you that couldn't be farther from the truth. I happen to have a delightfully wicked sense of humor. And as sick as I was feeling, I was thoroughly entertained at the sight of her trying to get up.

Her knee had given out so suddenly that her walking stick was of no use in balancing, and down she went. The weight of the pack had pulled her onto her back, making her look like an overturned beetle as she flailed her arms and legs trying to right herself. It took her a few moments to realize she had to release the pack before she could succeed.

There was a creek that ran adjacent to the path now and, at times, I was able to access it but it was of no use to her. So, again, she ran out of water but a couple of cyclists, without her asking, poured their icy water into my lady's bottle as they passed us on the trail. They had just come through a town and said we had another two miles to go.

When we got there, I slumped down in the shade outside a grocery store. My lady dropped the bag, poured me the last of the cool water, and walked into the store as I lay in the doorway. A woman immediately walked over to her; she grabbed a chair and gently eased my lady into it then ran over to the cooler and got a bottle of green liquid.

"Here honey, sip this slowly," she said, and then asked a co-worker to get some wet paper towels from the restroom. My lady didn't speak for a long while; she just sat there panting, sipping the cold liquid and patting her surprisingly dry, dark red, face with wet paper towels.

"Have you eaten? Do you need a place to stay?" And then, "What are you doing out there in this heat, anyway? It's 111 degrees! Do you want to kill yourself--and that dog? And, you're a woman walking alone out here? Do you have any idea how dangerous that can be? Do you know women have disappeared on this trail?"

My lady asked if there was a vet in town, someone that she could talk to about me. Once she explained my symptoms, the lady she spoke to on the phone informed her that I was having a heat stroke. The remedy was simple--"electrolytes, and a lot of water and rest."

The woman that worked at the store made a few phone calls and returned to us. She said she had called the police station and gotten permission for us to stay in the public park.

"There are trees and a swimming pool. And there's a hose they will let you use to cool her off." She looked down at me and smiled. "You can stay for a few days, until you're well enough to travel." With that she handed my lady $25 and went back to work, shushing her as she tried to express her thanks.

An hour later we were well enough to walk the few blocks to the park. My lady put up the tent under a large tree and we slept all day. Waking up briefly, we'd walk over to the hose and she'd soak me down and run water over the back of her neck and head, and then we'd go back to sleep.

She coerced me frequently, but I just did not want to drink any water. My head hurt when I lifted it, and the water all tasted funny to me and made me feel sick. Then she mixed something in it, from a package she pulled from the backpack. She called it "miso;" it smelled like seaweed and tasted delicious so I slowly lapped it up. The second day, she went to the store while I lay there with a couple of children we had met earlier, and came back with a couple of cans of tuna fish. Opening one of them, she drained some of the water into a bowl, diluting it with plain water. Again, she tricked me into drinking.

I could feel our walk was coming to an end. I think she felt it, too. Yet, she planned one final attempt before she was willing to stop. Once we were able to move on, she stuck out her thumb and we were picked up by an older man with a very large white dog named Bo. Fortunately, Bo was very hairy and very hot; he had no desire to even greet me, let alone object, as I got into the front and sat on the floor between my lady's legs.

As he dropped us off in Booneville, at a grocery store, the pudgy older man with the big cowboy hat handed her twenty dollars, "to help out on the road."

"I'll make it forty if you want to come down to the river and give me some lovin'," he added, licking his lips.

"Wow." I could tell she was taken completely off guard. "Thank you, but ... I'm pretty grungy from traveling, so I have to pass. Thank you, anyway," she stuttered as she backed out of the vehicle holding my collar so tight that I was having trouble breathing.

"Well, take this in case you change your mind." He handed her a business card which told her that he was the county commissioner. "Just don't call the home number; you don't need to be talking to my wife."

She just stood with her mouth open, holding the card as he drove away.

"He actually gave me his card, Ebby. He treated me like a whore, then he gave me his card."

A car pulled up behind her and beeped for us to move out of the way. When we got under the awning in front of the store she sat on some stacked bags of compost, and the tears began to flow. As much as she wiped her cheeks, she could not keep up with them. I could feel her frustration rising at her lack of control.

A large, dark-skinned woman in a floral print dress approached with two other similarly dressed women.

"Oh, what's the matter, honey," she asked as she handed my lady a tissue that she pulled from her bra. Between chokes and sobs and honks into the perfumed tissue, my human was able to tell them about the commissioner.

"Oh, he's such a dirty old man, the Lord'll take care of him one day. Rest assured, he will not be forgotten on the day of judgement! Don't you let him get to you."

They tried to lift her spirits and realized it was not working. So they gathered around her and held hands, talking to the sky like my lady does. They stayed around her, in a protective circle, patting her shoulder and fanning her with store advertisements, until she was able to gather herself together.

Apparently, this store didn't have what she was looking for, so we headed to another. After she was in the next store for a few minutes, she headed out the door, back to me. A woman that worked in the store followed her out and introduced herself.

"You walked in and I saw your tattoos and thought, 'Oh, they're not going to *get* her here.'" She laughed and told us that she was from California. "This place takes a long time to get used to and to be accepted in."

My lady was suddenly telling her what happened with the commissioner and about our health.

"Well, sounds like you need a place to recuperate and rethink." When she was off work, she brought us out to her home. It was an air-conditioned house with an amiable dog named Hershey and several horses out back, in a town called Prairie Home.

The women hit it off right away; they chatted and laughed like they had been friends for a very long time. It was wonderfully cool in the house as we recovered from the heat.

After purchasing a baby carriage for me *(I was so embarrassed!)* we had made one last attempt to walk, which failed miserably as the wheels collapsed in on themselves under the combined weight of the backpack, the water and me. So we returned to the house where my lady sat writing in her journal and talking earnestly with our hostess, I could feel her confusion and frustration. She said that she wanted to keep walking, but she could feel a pull back to the West Coast, where it was cool all the time, and where her son was living. Both of those things sounded wonderful to me.

We stayed for a few more days while my lady watched the woman's home and fed her horses as she took a weekend trip. My green-eyed human spent the time writing and talking to the sky, and when our hostess returned we left for the west coast.

****

CHAPTER SEVEN

"You! Oh, I bet you've been some great places," he exclaimed as he opened the car door for her and tossed the garbage from the front floor onto the already cluttered back seat. "You have to tell me stories on the ride over the hill. That's the fee for a ride in my chariot!"

We were very tired. It had been a long day traveling down Interstate 5, from Washington and down into California. This enthusiastic man had pulled over at the intersection of Highways 20 and 101, in Willits, on the way to the sweet-smelling Mendocino coast. He told my lady that he had followed the articles she had been writing for a newspaper in Booneville while we were walking, and was looking forward to hearing more. I could tell she was pleasantly surprised by the welcome. We had been gone for a year and had lost contact with most of the people we knew.

She told him of several amusing things that had happened as we traveled. One being the ride with the man with the funny accent.

He told my lady that he was a "Kiwi, from New Zealand" and called me, "Eeby." He was *huge*--not fat, just huge. I had never seen such a large human! He was easily three times the weight of my lady. They got along great during the three day drive to Portland, and there was much laughter. The fact was, many of the things they said weren't terribly funny, but they were both thoroughly and ridiculously amused by each other's accents.

We had spent the last three days with him and she had not been afraid at all. They had slept, head to toe, in his large bed in the cab of the truck. He slept under the covers and she slept on top of them in her sleeping bag. I could feel her discomfort at being pressed against the back wall of the cab when he'd turn in his sleep. But I know that she was also feeling very anxious about getting back to the coast where we'd be cool and where we could see her son.

The only time I sensed a change in the energy was on the last day, when he told her that he used to be employed by his government.

He explained that he had been an interrogator and had supposedly questioned a woman regarding the bombing of a ship called the Rainbow Warrior, which had ocurred off the coast of his homeland. I didn't know anything about what he was saying, but I did get a very clear sense that my lady's feelings changed toward him when he recounted his story. There were suddenly unmistakable smells of mistrust and a little fear, yet she manufactured smiles and polite comments for the remainder of the trip.

"I'm good at what I do. Somehow, with all her crying and pleading, I was completely unaffected, and just kept at her." The fact that I sensed strong feelings of remorse made me think that he just needed to tell someone, and my lady is a good listener. I could tell he meant her no harm--if he did, he had had plenty of opportunities to hurt us over the last few days as we drove through beautiful, yet vastly unpopulated, areas of Wisconsin and Montana. But she couldn't sense what I did, and I felt her confusion.

Our enthusiastic driver brought me back to the present.

"I live on a huge piece of land over in Clearlake. Once you are done on the coast you're welcome to stay until you decide where you're going next," he offered. "And I have some work you could do, if you want." He was odd, and tended to go off on a tangent as he chattered at my lady, but I didn't sense any danger.

He brought us directly to the address my lady had given him. I could feel unmistakable excitement coming from her; she was actually wriggling in her seat as we pulled into the driveway. She jumped out and ran to the man who had emerged from an apartment door as soon as the car came to a stop. Their hug was long and tight.

I was amused; my human does not like being touched, and certainly not hugged. Yet, through the years, I discovered that there were a very few select people that were able to safely breech that boundary. Without question, this man was one of them. He stood just a few inches taller than her. While her hair was cropped short again because we were traveling, his hair was tied behind his head and hung down to the middle of his back. He was not a large man; he was lean and muscular--and he smelled good. I didn't recognize the smell until later when they sat on the porch, and he pulled out what he called a clove cigarette for them to share.

After we said goodbye to the man who gave us the ride we went into the apartment with my lady's friend. I had never met this man before, but I could feel the love between them. As drained as she was, she was very happy to see him and seemed to get a second wind. This was one of the very few times, in many months, that I could feel her let her guard down. One thing I noticed was that the pepper spray remained in the backpack, instead of under her pillow, during the couple of nights we spent in his home.

"Oh, I've missed you so much," she said as she grabbed him and embraced him again. "And you still give the best hugs!"

The next morning we walked around the town that used to be our home. It felt good to be here; the familiar smells and cool, damp air were comforting. We stopped by the coffee house on Laurel Street.

LORI ELLEN BROCHHAGEN

I waited by the front door as my lady went in to get a drink. When she came out, she was with the man that drove us from Willits and two other men, who appeared to be friends with my human.

"Okay, so you're going to join us, right," our over-zealous driver asked. When she tentatively said yes, he got even more animated. "Music Festival on the Mendo Headlands! Oh baby, this is going to be great!" He did a little dance as he made his way to his car.

We walked out to Todd's Point to see the coastline. One thing that has always soothed my green-eyed lady is water. Whether it is the ocean or a lake, or a river, I can feel her anxiety seem to be carried away by the receding waves or by a river's current. The other thing that we *both* enjoy is my diving for rocks. She throws a rock into the water and I run, or sometimes swim, out to get it. I always try my best to bring back the one that she throws because it seems to make her so happy, and I enjoy the challenge.

The smell of the salt air was exhilarating! I chased seagulls as she sat quietly and seemed mesmerized by the undulating canvas of blue. We spent a relaxing day doing nothing at all--and it was wonderful. It was something we both desperately needed.

That evening we got to Mendocino early enough that we were able to walk around the town a bit. The first person we saw was a very tall man with long black dreadlocked hair. Sitting atop the matted mane was a dark blue knit cap. He recognized my lady immediately and smiled broadly, white teeth beaming from his dark face. He never remembered her name so he always called her "Ebony's mom." He reached down to pet me and his hand was so large that it completely covered my head.

We rounded the corner because my lady said she wanted to get something called "sea crunchies" from the red health food store. Almost at the store, a car screeched into a parking place, feet from where we stood, and came to an abrupt stop. The driver's door opened and a loud, laughing, hairy man emerged. I remembered him from when we lived here; he had given her a signed copy of his book of fables when we returned from our first leg of the journey.

"You are back! The coast of Mendocino is brighter because of your presence." He hugged her tightly. "Would you care to partake of some Rastafarian sacraments?"

She laughed and squirmed out of his embrace before accepting a toke from a rather large joint.

"So how are you," she asked as she let the smoke slowly seep from her lungs.

"I'm dying!"

This was his frequent response over the past few months, ever since he had been diagnosed with cancer. People usually reacted uncomfortably, not knowing how to respond. My lady just rolled her eyes, shook her head and smiled quietly.

They talked for a while; as he was walking away he turned, clasped his hands together in front of his chest, bowed to her and said, "Namaste."

Not long after, we sat at a picnic table listening to the words, "I'm crazy 'bout a Mercury" come wafting through the evening air. She kept slapping her neck and arms, and I had to keep flicking my ears to keep the mosquitoes from landing on them. Other than those pests, the evening was beautiful. It was warm enough for my lady to wear a thin-strapped, skimpy blue and black print dress. She had kept it rolled up at the bottom of the backpack "'cause you never know." Her eyes sparkled blue this evening, and it felt good to know she was relaxing for a change.

Then the quirky, enthusiastic man said, "Uh-oh."

He nodded to an erupting scene at the entrance to a tented entertainment area. There was a man standing there with a cigarette right below the "no smoking" sign, and there were two police officers asking him something. His back was to us but I could smell him, and her body tensing up told me that she recognized him too. He was yelling something at the officers. Their hand motions, and fingers to their lips, suggested that they just wanted him to be quiet and put the cigarette out, but he just seemed to want to yell.

"You come here to do your concerts; you fence everything off and make rules for us to follow! These headlands are my home, and you can't tell me what to do in my home!"

A woman came over to them, put an arm around his waist, and tried to cajole him away. He raised his arm--she flinched slightly-- and he put it around her shoulder as they turned and walked toward the exit, which was just past our table.

"Are you okay," her friends asked as they casually maneuvered to surround her, and as I sat up.

The man momentarily stumbled and his woman supported him as they walked past us. She looked directly at my lady and recognized her immediately, but remained silent. He seemed oblivious to our presence. As the two women looked in each other's eyes, one's gaze held embarrassment, the other's empathy.

Realizing that there was no threat to us, we both relaxed. My lady turned back to the music as the tension dissipated and a smile returned to her face.

"Oh, I'm fine," she chuckled and slapped at another mosquito, "this is perfect, just what I needed."

"Same as it ever was," one of the men shook his head as he offered her some repellant.

"I'm just so glad that's not me anymore," she said as she glanced, one more time, at the woman trying to calm the man that smelled bad.

The following day was perfectly enjoyable. Her son's dad brought him into town so we could spend the day together. I was so excited to see him that I peed a little. And, of course, my lady was ecstatic to see him. Our fifteen-year-old boy had grown and changed so much in the few months since we had seen him last. He was now a strong young man, but he still smelled like my boy.

We spent the day with the man that smelled like cloves and his son, and our boy. There was a lot of laughter and playing and story telling as these friends and family enjoyed their reunion. I sat in the car as they went in to eat and play some miniature golf; I could hear their laughter from the parking lot. On this occasion I was really wishing she would have brought me in; I was itching to chase after all those balls they were hitting! It didn't seem fair to me that I should have to sit out here and watch them play with, what were obviously, dog toys.

That evening, after the boys had gone out on their own, she and her friend sat and talked. Sometimes they laughed, a couple of times they cried. I could feel so many pent up emotions come flooding out of her.

After she told him about seeing her ex-husband at the concert, she acted like she suddenly remembered something.

"Oh, and I still owe you a kick in the nuts for introducing us." She pretended to frown.

"Hey, you could have just said no," he retorted.

She had been munching on a snickerdoodle and playfully tossed a piece at him. He swiped his hand to the side, sending it flying to the floor, conveniently close to my face. *Nice!* I crunched on it as they continued to talk.

"I'm not sure what to do. As much as I want to be near my son, I know I can't stay on the coast. But I don't know where to head, or even what to do with myself. Should I try to continue walking? The further east we got, the more danger we were in; it was actually getting scary. And we can't walk in the heat anymore. She can't take it; oh man, I was so worried about her in Missouri." She paused, reached down and rubbed behind my ears.

"I just feel completely directionless and unbalanced. I like Colorado more than California; there is much more free space in Colorado, but ... I don't know. Is it wrong to be so far from my son? I mean, he lives with his dad and seems to get everything he wants, which I'm happy about--to an extent! There was so much I couldn't give him. And it's not like we don't see each other; he flies out there, and I visit the coast. Is he better off with his dad so he has a male influence? Although, he's not really raising him; they're more like roommates. There are no restrictions, no rules, no responsibilities.

How is he going to be able to take care of himself when he's older if no one is teaching him now? And I have lived in that household before and, 'bless his heart,' to quote your mom, there are real reasons that I divorced that man. I still do not feel that it's the healthiest environment for him, but if I stay it could be embarrassing for him. I don't want him to be the kid in school with the homeless mom ..."

"Okay. Okay, stop." He held up his hand. "Take a breath."

He stood and came around behind her, as she sat at the table. She made a funny noise as he began to squeeze her shoulders with his strong hands. I could see the muscles and tendons in his arms work just under his skin as he massaged her.

"Hey, that hurts," she winced. "Ow ... oh, that's good."

"Your whole upper back and your shoulders are solid knots. Ya gotta learn to release that shit or it's gonna make you sick," he said as he dug into a particularly hard spot, making her cry out.

"Quiet your mind and the clarity will come. You know that." He slapped her playfully on the side of her head and walked to the fridge to get another ginger brew.

The next morning, after she said tearful goodbyes to her son and friend, the quirky man picked us up and drove us to Clearlake. The property was beautiful. It was right on the lake, and there was a row boat tied up, ready for launch--which seemed to thrill my lady.

"This is pretty sweet!"

Later that day, we were relaxing in the shaded tent, listening to the water lapping on the bank of the lake. I walked over to the sprinkler and drank some water. As I was getting back into the tent, I heard an odd squeal. Turning around I saw that the very thin, quirky man--clad in only a red bikini bottom--had emerged from the path that led to his home, and had leapt through the sprinkler. His gray pony tail was plastered to his wet back as he giggled and danced in and out of the streams of water. I heard a muffled snort from behind me and turned. My lady had seen him also and had toppled over onto the sleeping bag, and out of his view, as she held her hands over her mouth, trying to stifle her laughter.

She calmed herself and sat up, but when our eyes met she fell back into another fit of hysterics. It took a few minutes for her to compose herself enough for us to walk past the man, get into the row boat and cast off.

I was, most definitely, not comfortable with this new situation. I tried to balance as the bottom of the boat kept moving beneath my feet. I was unsuccessful and landed on my side with a grunt, which sent her into yet another fit of hysterical laughter. Remaining in a horizontal position for the remainder of this horrible excursion seemed prudent. I just wished it would stop rocking. There was a sick feeling in my stomach, and I was glad I had not eaten dinner yet.

"Oh, are you not liking this, Ebony," she asked with mock concern. "It's okay, you're safe. We're heading back now. It'll be just a few more minutes, ya big baby," she laughed.

Until we were on solid, non-moving, ground I amused myself thinking about revenge. I thought about the small tent, and hoped that it was turkey for dinner tonight, which produces the most noxious farts.

We spent a few days on the property as she did her best to avoid the quirky, dancing man. When he chattered at her, I could feel her tense up slightly.

"Oh man, Ebby! His talking is just like jazz music." She slapped her hands to her ears.

She wound up being restless and unsettled during most of our stay in Clearlake. So from there we went to Willits to spend some time with another close friend. I liked this lady, and I liked the way she spoke; her voice was musical to me. She had told my lady she was from a far away place called Denmark.

This woman had lived in Mendocino, next to the grocery store where my human had worked for almost a year, and had let us park in her driveway for several months, giving us a place to sleep. It had felt safe since the man who smelled bad was living in Ft. Bragg at the time, and the stolen van had long since stopped running.

This lady with the musical voice had been looking for a person to rent an extra room in her home; however, that didn't work out because the lady was afraid that I'd scare her cat. I do enjoy chasing cats--and they always start it. I mean, I can ignore them just fine. Then they give me that look. It's a challenge, plain and simple, which must be accepted.

Weeks later we were still in the van, the police were still knocking on the window at night and asking us to move somewhere else, and the man that smelled bad still managed to threaten my lady almost every day when she went to work. So she had knocked on the musical-voiced lady's door and told her our situation. The woman's smile was warm and she spoke softly. She told my human she could park in her driveway and plug a cord into her house so that we could watch videos at night. We were able to stay there until the man found out where we were parking and we had to move elsewhere, so as not to cause problems for our friend from Denmark.

Over the past couple of years my human and the lady with the musical voice visited with each other occasionally, and a slow, strong friendship developed. At times we would arrive at her home when my lady was feeling intense anxiety and fear; they would sit and drink tea as the room would fill with tobacco and cannabis smoke, and as they spoke, I could feel her become calm and more clear.

And now we were at the woman's new home in Willits. It was another place that I enjoyed, like that house in Placerville; there were no offensive noises or smells. Solar energy powered everything on the land and redwood trees surrounded this peaceful sanctuary. The soft-spoken woman with the musical accent had a huge tent in which we stayed for over a week. There were large cushions and screened, zippered windows on all four sides; we were safe from the bugs, but we were outside--perfect. Titter, her small, elderly cat, stayed inside until she knew that I was zipped into the tent. I didn't want to chase her anyway; it takes the fun out of the chase when they are actually afraid of me.

When she wasn't sitting quietly, staring into the trees, my lady was filling bottles with herbal lotions made by her friend. The room in which she filled them was in the main house, where the person that owned the property lived. It was open on one side, to the forest. At pretty much every turn, we were surrounded by trees, which seemed to absorb the anxiety and confusion from my lady.

"Are you writing yet," asked the woman with the soft voice as they prepared dinner. "That's what you need to be doing. And you need to do it away from here, far away from here. Go back to Colorado. He's not stable--neither are you, for that matter. And just because he didn't notice you at the concert doesn't mean he won't when he has a sober moment."

"Yeah, like he has those anymore," she chuckled, yet there was no smile in her eyes. She took a long drag off of her cigarette; as she released it she shrugged, "You're right ..."

"Of course I am. You really shouldn't be here where he can get at you," she shook her head and made a face like she might be sick. "Oh, I honestly don't know how you ever let him touch you. He's so gross, and you *kissed* him." She grabbed her own throat and gagged dramatically.

"Okay, okay! I get it," my lady snapped, then she looked at the other woman, and they both burst into laughter. When the laughter subsided my human continued.

"You don't know how I saw him when we first met. I thought he was amazing; he seemed so beautiful, like the guy I've always been looking for. He always said and did the perfect things, and he treated me the way I always thought I wanted to be treated. But it just turned out to be a really good con." She took a deep breath. "By the time I realized ..." her voice trailed off and her face went blank as she stared past her friend, who noisily dropped a pan on the counter and watched with a grin as my lady snapped back to the present. She waved her middle finger at her friend and continued.

"The best thing is for me to be alone for now. I'm over forty years old and I still have no idea what I want to do when I grow up. My whole life, I've never been alone, and I have always wanted whatever the guy in my life wanted; I don't even know what my favorite color is. When I fall in love, I become an insane person, absolutely incapable of making a rational decision. Man, I've made some *really* stupid mistakes; but, that dosn't change the fact that men suck." She exhaled angrily and smashed her cigarette in the ashtray.

"Seriously, they suck the life right out of me."

"That's because you let them ..." Her friend with the musical voice was about to say more when she saw my lady's face. The tears had begun to flow and it would be almost an hour before they would stop. Our hostess gave her tissues and quietly continued to fix dinner.

****

Chapter Eight

*W*ithin a few days of arriving in Salida, Colorado, my lady had gotten a job as a dishwasher at a pancake restaurant on Highway 50, and several days after that, one of the waitresses let us stay in an extra room in her home, which was located next to a stockyard full of cows.

Before we moved into that room, we were in the tent and I would go to work with her and stay outside the back door while she washed dishes. She and the waitresses would come out frequently to play with me and sneak me food. There was also another dishwasher there, a tall man with large hands, who seemed to like to hang out with me whenever he had a break.

Each day after work she sat rubbing her wrists together, and sometimes the pain made her cry. She told the waitress we were staying with that it was just because the dishes were so heavy, and that it would pass as she got stronger.

The young couple that had taken us in was nice and my lady was very grateful. Mountain nights were cold, and she had begun to feel achy in the chilly mornings. Since she was working, she said it was important to live indoors, where she could shower and stay clean.

There were two things I didn't like about the place, however. One was Max, a very large rottwheiler bitch, who took my toy and refused to relinquish it even when my lady attempted get it back. Before the dog's human could intervene, she had ripped it to shreds.

The other was the stench. There was the sickly, sour smell of fear emanating from the muddy stock yard and it permeated everything. I don't know how it didn't bother the other people living in the vicinity. How could they go about their lives, laughing and playing, when right outside their windows, these animals were suffering? Could they not sense it, or did they not care?

Those cows knew where they were and where the truck was going to take them when it carried them away. I felt their anxiety, and so did my lady. We would walk out to the yard and she'd pick up some loose hay and feed it to the cows through the fence. She'd tell them that they were beautiful and how sorry she was for what was happening. When they were being driven away, we could see their wide eyes peering through the slats of the trucks; I will never forget that image. Tears rolled down her face, and I could feel her self-restraint, as she watched them being driven off.

"I hate that there's nothing I can do to stop them. I could lie in front of the truck," she mused, "but they'd just call the cops and move me out of the way. Then it'd be business as usual."

I could feel how deeply she was affected by other creatures' suffering; it was something that profoundly disturbed her. There were several times when she approached someone and intervened when she saw a dog being abused or a child being treated poorly. It truly seemed to be involuntary, like she just couldn't stop herself.

One day, outside the laundromat in the shopping center in Fort Bragg, my lady was getting out of the truck to go in and fold her clothes, when we both heard a child scream and the sound of slapping. She left the door open as I climbed into the driver's seat. I could feel her hesitation as she quietly shook her head.

When the child cried louder she said, "Shit."

I leaned out and watched her approach a woman holding the arm of a small girl.

"Hey! Why don't you pick on someone closer to your size," my lady asked loudly. Frankly, I don't know what she would have done if the woman had actually chosen to hit her instead of the little girl; I had never seen her fight with anyone, and I wasn't even sure that she was able.

"She ran out in front of a car." The woman defended herself, then snapped back, "Hey, mind your own fucking business, anyway!"

"It is my business," she stated matter-of-factly.

She glanced over at the four men standing at the entrance to the laundromat and raised her voice, "it's *all* of our business! It's never okay to hit a kid! You're just being a bully!"

My lady then walked back and shut the truck door, but I could still see and hear her as she walked to the door to get her laundry. As she passed the men she stopped.

Oh great, and I couldn't get out to help her.

"And you! You guys just stood there and watched."

The men stood there with their mouths open and watched her enter the laundromat. I watched as they remained silent, even after she went in, and stared hard at the tips of their cigarettes as they made them glow.

Anyway, we were both relieved when we met with the woman who managed some apartments on Sackett Avenue, one block from the Arkansas River that I enjoyed so much. I could hear my lady talk to her on the phone before we met at the apartment building. The woman said that she wouldn't allow pets in the building.

"Oh, but Ebony is a very good dog. I can give you better references for her than I can for myself."

"Yeah, I don't know if it's a good idea to be telling me that." I could hear the woman laugh through the speaker.

When we met her in front of the apartment building, I liked her right away. She smelled good, like bread baking, or coffee brewing; the manager's scent was similar to the aroma that had attracted me to my lady when we first met.

The woman bent down to say hello to me. I grabbed a leaf from the ground and brought it to her; just as she was about to take it I whipped around and presented her with my wriggling hind quarters.

"It's a trick," my lady laughed. "She lures you in with a ball or a leaf then turns around so you can scratch her back--not too subtle." As the lady scratched my back vigorously, she shook her head and added, "But it always seems to work."

The good-smelling apartment manager brought us into three empty apartments. When we entered the last one, the one on the second floor with a balcony and a perfect view of Tenderfoot Hill, my lady made her choice. There were two rooms in this apartment, a kitchen and a "bedroom-slash-living room." The street side had tall, heavy windows in both rooms; through them we would watch fireworks bursting over the mountain on the Fourth of July and the day after Thanksgiving. On that Friday after Thanksgiving there was a parade each year that ended at the parking lot past the F Street bridge, near the base of the hill that was often called S Mountain because of the huge white S on it. Then, with a great deal of fan fare, the entire hill, which was strewn with colored lights, was lit up. From a distance it looked like a gigantic decorated holiday tree. Then the fireworks started. In July, we would join the other neighbors out on the roof and watch from there, but would take advantage of the tall windows in the winter, staying nice and cozy as we enjoyed the show.

"Oh wow, it's a little hobbit bathroom," she laughed as she peeked her head into the closet-sized room containing a toilet, mini sink and tiny shower stall.

I, of course, won the heart of the good-smelling lady and she told us we could move in right away if we liked.

When my lady wasn't at work, she busied herself with decorating--and redecorating--our home. Until she lay down to go to sleep, she was moving. If she was sitting, she was doing puzzles or drawing, or writing in a notebook--and her leg was constantly shaking. No matter what, she always seemed busy. We also went to the river a lot. The only time she seemed to stop was when she'd sit on the bank and watch me pull rocks from the current; and, that was the only time she seemed to be relaxed.

As we'd leave the river I would, invariably, carry one of the rocks home with me. There was a nice pile accumulating on the floor near my bed. Sometimes, people would ask why my lady let me keep them inside.

"I figure if she takes the trouble to carry it all the way home, she deserves to keep it."

One of the neighbors had donated a large, round, "seventies-style" lounge to our new home. It immediately became my bed, my throne. She situated it in the corner of the room, right under a window. I could stretch out in comfort as I rested my chin on the window sill, listened to the river, and watched the people go travel by on the street below.

The neighbors were nice. A few of them were a bit quirky, but they all smelled like good people. There was the lady who lived below us in one of the larger apartments. She was very thin and didn't smell healthy; there was an illness inside of her. As nice as she was, she was definitely one of the quirky people. She kept bright pink signs in her front window, saying that the government had stolen her child, and below the window on the sidewalk, was a full-sized white porcelain toilet--which she used for a flower planter.

One afternoon, we came home from the library to find that she had emptied her apartment of all of its contents and placed them neatly in the courtyard.

"Hi," my lady said with a huge smile. "Whatcha doin'?"

"There's a bug in my apartment," she panted.

"Wow, musta been a big one." My lady laughed but I could feel her insistence that we continue to walk up the path to the stairs. To me she whispered, *I thought I was bad.*

"No, they are very tiny." She slammed her fist onto the picnic table. "I know they put one in my apartment when they were 'checking for gas leaks' last month." She crooked her fingers and made quotation marks in the air. "They have been listening for a while now ... but," she smiled, came closer and almost whispered, "I'm smarter than they are. I never talk on the phone when I'm inside, and I memorize and burn all my notes and receipts. And I *never* use a computer in my home."

"Oh, *that* kind of bug! Okay, so it's gonna rain soon; did you find it yet? I mean, do you want help getting this stuff back inside?"

"No! And no, thank you."

Just then, another of our neighbors rode up on his bicycle. He stood there, straddling his bike and shaking his head; then he bent down low to greet me, I'm guessing so that the quirky woman wouldn't see him trying not to smirk. He and she had been friends for awhile apparently, so once he was in control of his face, he leaned his bike up against a tree and began to carry her furniture back inside while she yelled at him to stop. When she hit him in the back of the head with a stuffed purple elephant, my lady shook her head and we continued up the stairs and into our apartment.

The police came; the good-smelling manager came; the neighbors came. We went back out and stood at the top of the stairs and watched as they all convinced our downstairs neighbor that, listening devices or no, her furniture and possessions must go back inside. Even the officers helped as the rain began. I was surprised; the police seemed to be nice here.

"I should've made some popcorn," my human laughed.

We went back inside and she flopped down onto the futon, still snickering. A few days before that we had met two other men that lived here. One was a small, bent, old-looking man with white, thinning hair and a beard. The other was a much larger man with very little hair on the top of his head, but a long white beard hanging from his face. The two men would sit in the courtyard and drink beer. When they had had too much, usually each evening, they would begin to argue "like an old married couple," she said. This sometimes included wrestling in the dust near the fire pit, and always culminated in them slamming their doors as they stormed into their respective apartments. The next morning they would come out and sit at the picnic table and drink coffee, speaking in barely audible mutters. If it was warm, my lady would leave our door open. I liked to wander out and sit on the deck in the shade of a tree and look down on the comical scenes that unfolded in our neighborhood.

It was nearing the end of fall when my lady left the job at the pancake place for a position, as a barista, at the cafe which was a block down the street from our apartment. It was a coffee house that served food and wine, and had live music each weekend; it was the place that had let my lady set up a table to talk to people when we were here on the second leg of the trek. She had applied months ago and checked in with them regularly as she waited for an opening. I could feel her relief at not having to wash those dishes anymore; the pain in her wrists did not diminish as she had hoped. Also, she said she was glad she didn't have to ride the brakeless bike, that someone had given her, to work each day at 5:40 a.m. She laughed, saying that it was fine going to work because it was all up hill; however, coming back she had to "run into a curb a couple of times to stop" when there was traffic on D Street.

Although she was always tired when she got home, I sensed that she liked her job very much. And I liked that she worked there because she brought home all kinds of foods. Also, she came home to let me out on her break since she was so close.

Since we were only a block away, other employees would stop by sometimes before or after work. It was fun having people visit. The apartment was very small, so sometimes I had to relinquish my throne so that a couple of humans could sit. Downstairs lived a man who played the guitar and sang; sometimes he and a couple of other people would come over to play music and laugh and talk until the middle of the night.

My lady had been alone, except for me, for a little while now, and it pleased me to see her with other people. It was nice that she was smiling more. Things weren't *great* for her though. I could sense her struggle to stay in control of the anxiety that sometimes overtook her. There were certain sounds that would cause her to become irritable, and we lived in what seemed to be the noisiest area of the entire town.

Within two blocks there were four bars that all played live music on the weekends. And all those bars, plus several restaurants got daily deliveries of food and alcohol, which arrived in large, noisy, smelly trucks; then all that waste had to be hauled away in garbage trucks. They were joined by snow plows, leaf blowers, skateboards and street sweepers.

There were also occasions, I must say, when I didn't hear anything- -yet she would swear she heard a motor running. Sometimes she'd wear ear plugs; that seemed to help a little. Sometimes she'd turn on some music. Other times, nothing would work, and she would succumb to the anxiety and pull herself into a ball and surround herself with blankets and pillows on the closet floor and rock herself to sleep.

The street sweeper came on Fridays at 4:10 a.m. With our large windows that faced the street, noise amplified by the time it rose to our level. My lady was usually awake at that hour, listening to the British news and doing puzzles. That noise would set her to pacing and becoming agitated. One morning she decided to "adjust her attitude," she said. Instead of getting angry, she chose to do something that would make her laugh.

So at 4:05, she turned out all the lights and opened the door; I sat in the kitchen doorway and watched her. Once outside, she placed a carton of eggs on the railing as she climbed over it and onto the roof of the first floor. She stood back from the edge and when the sweeper drove by she began hurling eggs onto the vehicle. Many times she missed, but when she hit him, and the eggs slid down his windshield, she squealed and quickly climbed back onto the deck and into the doorway, closing the door behind her. She'd slide down to the floor, breathlessly leaning against the door and laughing like a teenager who'd just gotten away with a great prank, as we listened to the driver yell obscenities in our direction. And, it worked; the anxiety was gone.

Once the weather started getting nice, we'd go over to the cafe in the evenings and sit by the river as we listened to music. It had been a long cold winter, and it had lasted far past when the radio said that spring should have started. But now the trees were getting new leaves and we went for more walks along the river and through the paths that wound around and behind S Mountain.

One of the other baristas, a new friend of my lady's, stopped by on the way to work so they could chat as they walked. As my lady put her jacket on and was saying goodbye to me she received a text on her phone. The color drained from her face as she felt for the chair and slumped into it.

"What's the matter," her friend asked when she saw her face. My lady handed her the phone so she could read what was on the screen.

"Sackett Avenue Whore, who's at your door?" She frowned and returned the phone. "Wow, that's pretty creepy. Do you know who it's from?"

I could feel the fear come from nowhere, and everywhere, bleeding through the cracks of her well-fortified sanctuary and instantly enveloping her. She couldn't speak for a moment. Her eyes were wide. I walked over and put my head in her lap. She put her hand on my head and suddenly inhaled, as if she had forgotten to breathe for those moments.

"My ex-husband; he's kind of insane."

****

CHAPTER NINE

"*He* was punching her and then he started choking her," her friend exclaimed to her boyfriend, who had just arrived, as she got some ice from the freezer. "The bouncer, you know, the one with the mohawk and the eyeliner, pulls him off her and keeps him in a bear hug until he calms down. He was awesome!"

She wrapped the ice in a towel and held it to my lady's swelling jaw and cheekbone; angry looking red marks laced her throat.

I liked this young woman. My green-eyed human had met her over at the cafe where they both made coffee drinks. The first time I saw her her short, wild, reddish hair looked so crazy it made me chuckle. Her boyfriend also worked at the cafe, cooking food. He was tall with light blonde hair that stuck up just like the woman's, and he always smelled yummy when he got off work.

"It all happened so fast, by the time I got through the crowd it was done." My lady's crazy-haired friend continued, but her boyfriend interrupted.

"Start from the beginning," he said. As her friend told us what happened, I sat with my head in my lady's lap. She was quiet, and she smelled of alcohol, cigarettes--and *the man who smelled bad.*

"We waited for two weeks to see that band. They were hot and we were dancing with a couple of guys. We were having so much fun. She was dancing with the guy from that conservation group, the cute one with the curly dark hair. You should have seen them! They looked so hot together ..." she stopped when he cleared his throat loudly.

"Okay, sorry! We left and walked around the block to get some fresh air 'cause it was so hot in there. When we turn back onto F Street, we hear, 'There she is!' And this cop comes walking up to us. He asks were we've been, like it's any of his business, and he says that there was a report that she had been stealing handbags from the bar ..."

At that moment my lady pulled out of her trance.

"Seriously! I was like, 'Are you *kidding* me?' I wasn't even carrying a bag of my own so I threw up my arms and spun around, 'Do I *look* like I'm stealing stuff? Wanna frisk me?' Then I looked at the pad he was writing in. And there at the top of the page, was his name, right there in big fucking letters.

"I looked toward the bar, and there he was, sitting on the curb! He was the one that yelled, 'there she is,'" she took a drag off of her cigarette and rearranged the icepack. "I told the cop that he was my ex-husband and that he must have seen me in there dancing and gotten jealous."

She said he stopped writing, then told them they were free to go as he put his pad and pen back in his pocket and headed for the drunken guy sitting on the curb.

"I was like, 'Hey, wait a minute! Is that it? No apology? You gonna arrest him for making a false police report?'"

"Why didn't you mention the restraining order," asked the tall blonde man, "he'd probably be in jail right now."

"I don't know ... I forgot." She huffed and rolled her eyes. "I'm kinda drunk, and I was surprised. Shut up!"

"Okay, okay." He put up his hands in mock surrender.

"*Anyway*," said my lady's friend loudly, clearly indignant at being interrupted. "I tried to shut her up as I pulled her with me, and we took another walk around the block so she'd cool off. It didn't work; she was really pissed. The whole time she's going, 'He's here! Why is he here?' When we got back the cop was gone and so was her ex, we thought, so we went back in for one more drink. But asshole was in there, sitting at a table with three of the bar skanks, and this one," nodding to my lady, "just went totally ballistic. She walked up to him and started yelling.

"'This is *my* home! You don't get to do this crap here! I have friends here and I'm not afraid of you anymore!" She paused and laughed. "You called the cops on me 'cause I was dancing with a guy? You know what? You are a fucking wet-brained lunatic! Why are you even *here*??'

"She was great! But then he grabbed a bunch of her hair as he stood, and was holding her tight so she couldn't move. He was smiling this creepy smile as he said something in her ear. Then he just started punching her! By the time I could get to her, the bouncer had a hold of him. When I asked him if he was gonna call the cops he said that they'd be here all the time if he did that every time a fight broke out, so he just got to leave!"

"I can't believe he's really here. Why? Is it possible that he came a thousand miles just to hurt me? Is that possible," she wondered out loud as she shook her head and scratched behind my ears.

"What did he say in your ear, anyway," her friend asked. My lady walked over to the sink and tossed the melting ice.

"Nothing."

"Tell us!" Her friends chimed in unison.

"He's such an asshole." She rolled her eyes and breathed deep. "When he was in prison, I had written him a poem; it said that I would love him always, and all ways," she paused and smiled weakly at her friends. "When he got drunk and mad at me he changed the words, saying that that was when and how he'd *hurt* me. So that's what he whispered, 'always, all ways'".

For the next few days my lady and I were not alone, as her friend spent each night at our place. That weekend several of her friends came over and we all hung around until quite late. It was a warm evening, so the kitchen door was open to the balcony. As my lady, her crazy-haired friend and I stood on the balcony, they looked down and across the street to where there was a garbage dumpster. Right behind it, yet in plain view as the street light was directly above him, crouched her ex-husband. I put my paws on the railing so I could see better. From my angle all I could see was the top of his head, but I could smell the festering stench of him.

"Um, we can see you," my lady yelled down to him, and she laughed out loud. "You look like Kilroy!" Make-up covered the purple bruises on her face and neck that were now tinged with yellow and she winced as she opened her mouth widely to laugh.

"He's loving the attention. Let's go back inside," said her friend to my lady, and as we went in she called over her shoulder to the man. "You're kind of creepy dude, why don't you go stalk someone else? This place is defended!"

"This place is defended," my lady asked when they were inside and the door was closed. "What the hell does that mean?"

"I don't know, I heard somebody say it in a movie. Sounded good when he said it. Listen, I don't like them either, but why don't you call the cops?"

"Because they never do anything. I have a restraining order; do you think that ever stopped him? It meant nothing!"

When it was clear that he was going to continue lurking, her friend with the crazy hair insisted that we stay with her and her tall blonde boyfriend at their place. She objected, saying that she wanted to protect her home; she didn't want him to break in and trash the place.

"I don't have very much any more, but it's all in here! I can't let him ruin anything else!"

"Better he trash your place than you," she said, and then made a face as though she wished she hadn't.

"Did you hear that in a movie too," my lady asked.

"Shut up and pack a bag; you're coming with us, and don't forget Ebony's bowls. I like her, but I don't want her sliming my dishes. No offense, dog," she said as she looked down at me. I was too unnerved by the situation to be offended.

The following day we all returned to the apartment to find that flower pots that once sat on the railing had been smashed on the street below, the window screen had been cut, and there were nicks in the wood around the door knob. I put my nose to the fresh stain on the door; it was definitely his urine. When my lady saw the stain, which was too high for even a large dog, and said, "Oh my god," it was clear that she knew what happened, too.

Both women were scheduled for work, and since they could see the apartment and it's door from the cafe, they felt it was okay to leave me home as they went to work.

Not fifteen minutes later I was laying on my throne, looking out the window, when a police car passed the apartment heading for the cafe with it's lights flashing. When the car stopped, two officers got out and went inside. Shortly afterward, I saw the officers emerge and between them, with his hands cuffed behind his back, was the man that smelled bad.

****

Chapter Ten

"*D*oes her being here make you feel more comfortable," the therapist asked my lady as she reached down and patted my head gently.

"Yes, I don't really go anywhere without her; thank you for letting me bring her in," she said to the other woman.

The therapist was pretty, with short, dark hair sprinkled with just a little bit of white, and warm brown eyes. I felt very relaxed laying there beside her.

Even though this woman felt unimposing and completely safe, I was on guard because I could feel my human's intense anxiety. I sat next to the therapist, and across from my lady so I could watch her without craning my neck, and so I could easily get between the two women if need be. Also, my beautiful green-eyed lady smelled bad.

Hygiene was not the issue, and I don't think any humans were able to sense it; that festering smell, the one that rose from deep within her, had overwhelmed the aroma that I loved so much about her.

Her five foot three inch frame now supported over 170 pounds, and her green eyes, rarely sparkled anymore. She cried a lot--sometimes because she was sad, sometimes because she was in physical pain. I was frustrated because, no matter how many rocks I pulled from the river, no matter how many snowballs I caught, and no matter how many times I did what she calls my "happy dog dance" (which was really just me flopping down on the ground and wriggling as I try to scratch that unreachable spot on my back) her smiles and laughs were brief. And then her eyes would cloud over again.

Lately, I had become much more protective of her, as she frequently seemed very vulnerable and afraid. It had been almost two years since the man that smelled bad had been here and gone back to California. Conversations between her and her friend with the crazy hair told me that once they got to work that day long ago, the cook pulled my lady into the kitchen and told her that her ex-husband was sitting at a table. Seeing her face, they said he had immediately called the police. Her ex-husband spent two weeks in jail; afterward he was here for a month or so sitting across the river playing his drum or sitting at a picnic table in the park watching the apartment. A woman who said she was his probation officer told my human, one afternoon, that he had called to inform her that he had returned to the Mendocino Coast. And that was that; apparently, sometimes even humans can not explain how or why people do things.

Almost all of our furnishings came from the thrift store on Fourth Street; everything was clean, but nothing was new. The apartment was all color-coordinated, always clean and very orderly. Everything had its place. Evenly spaced pottery vases and pitchers lined a high ledge on the wall facing the windows; pillows were precisely layered on the futon. Sometimes my lady would be watching a DVD and she'd pause it, get out the step stool and climb up to move a nic nac an inch to the right or left, then return to the movie. Other times she'd start moving furniture around before she could relax and finish her show. She would sit and stand in different parts of the small apartment to make sure that things looked pleasing no matter where one sat. She even made sure it looked good from my throne, which did not go unappreciated. She'd keep at it until everything felt comfortable and "balanced." It was also important for everything to have a place because of the problems she experienced with her memory, and not being able to find something was another cause for her bursts of rage.

Even though our home was always ready for visitors, there was never anyone over to see it. Her friends had moved or gotten different jobs, and my lady did not go out unless it was necessary, so she didn't make new friends. We went to the grocery store, the library, the river, and now, the therapist's office. There were some occasions when we went to the post office, the bank or the medical clinic; otherwise, we were either inside or sitting on the deck, or in the courtyard so I could play and she could get some fresh air.

Most of her time was spent at the kitchen table. She rarely slept more than three hours at a time, so we were usually up at about two or three in the morning. I happened to like this since it meant more attention, more pee breaks and, sometimes, more snacks. The radio was always on during the early hours and she reminded me, eerily, of the man that smelled bad. She listened to the news, drank a lot of coffee and smoked a lot cigarettes, and she either wrote in one book or drew pictures in another.

My lady was fired from the cafe because she said she made an "unnecessary" comment to her boss one day, so she began working at the tavern about a block in the other direction. After a few months, she was fired from there because she yelled at a drunken regular because he kept using the "N word," whatever that is. As she attempted to find another job, she did housekeeping jobs, and she cared for children while their parents went out. She awoke to pain in her upper body after laying down for those few hours each night, which brought her to tears almost every time. She kept losing her balance, so it was necessary for her to walk with a stick to steady herself. It hurt to be with her sometimes; the depression, anxiety and rage were all so intense.

There were times when we'd finally make it to the grocery store, which was only three blocks away, and I would be waiting outside for her. I wished she'd bring me in so I could help her stay relaxed. Many times, a nudge from me was all that was needed for her to be able to calm herself or remember to breathe. Sometimes I could hear her yelling angrily, through the open door, before she came storming out. Sometimes she would go in and be in there for a longer time than usual and she'd come out empty-handed, holding her chest and trying to slow her breathing before we'd hurry back to the apartment.

The quirky woman from downstairs moved out and another lady moved in. The first time we saw our new neighbor was in the courtyard. She was sitting at the picnic table and had just turned off her oxygen tank and removed the hose that attached to her nose, to light a cigarette. Her thick chestnut hair hung almost down to her waist and she had a contagious smile. This woman had a dog named Choowii. He was young, less than two when we met.

Both women suffered from similar physical ailments and emotional anxieties; and both of us dogs could see that they needed each other's friendship right now. So once her dog and I got to know each other, we worked to get our humans together. Neither of them liked going out in public. So we worked together to draw them out to the courtyard. When I'd hear him outside, I'd stand at the door and wag my tail. It didn't take my lady long to catch on that I didn't always have to pee when I wanted to go outside, so she'd usually grab her coffee and cigarettes and follow me out. His lady said that he did the same thing when he heard me.

On a particularly painful and anxiety-ridden morning, my lady sat with Choowii's human and cried from the pain in her shoulders. Then she held her head in her hands and frowned deeply.

"Are you okay? What's going on," our neighbor asked with concern.

"Those motors are driving me crazy," she said.

Her new friend listened for a moment, then shook her head.

"I don't hear anything; sounds pretty quiet to me."

"You can't hear that? I hear a motor, someone's running something," my lady cried.

"Wow, you really need to get to a doctor," she shook her head and thought a moment. "Look, you need help. Maybe your arthritis has gotten worse, maybe it's fibromyalgia or the carpal tunnel. Who knows? Whatever it is, they have tests and can find out. And then you need to get to a shrink. Someone that can help you to process all that crap in your head, and help you relax a little."

When my lady looked at her as if she couldn't understand her words, she tried again.

"Okay. First things first; make an appointment at the medical clinic. Can you do that," she asked.

"I guess. I don't know. I don't have insurance, so they'll just try to give me some crap medications and send me on my way. I've been through all that in California, one of my friends actually died because of the clinics out there; and I was on my way to the same end. I'm not going there again."

"Well, this is not Ft. Bragg-freakin-California. Just take a breath, make an appointment, then go from there. It's important to take some kind of step, then everything will fall into place." My lady did not respond; she just reached down, grabbed a small stick and threw it for me to chase.

"Okay?"

"Okay!"

When they finished their coffee, my human went upstairs and called the clinic. The next morning she showered and went out early, taking her bike--not the brakeless one; she now had a pretty gold bike that she called Betsy--so I stayed home. When she returned, she came upstairs and made some tea, and we went outside to sit with Choowii and his lady.

"There was an actual doctor there; that was cool. He poked and prodded and asked a bunch of questions. Then he told me that I have fibromyalgia. I gotta say, it's a relief to know that; I thought I was just a serious pussy when it came to pain. I'd get a massage or a neck rub or something and I'd be flinching all over the place. That's one reason I don't like being touched; it's just always so uncomfortable.

"He said there's also a re-occurence of the carpal tunnel; can you believe that? I had surgery and it came back! I have arthritis in my knees, ankles, elbows and hands. Most of the back pain seems to be coming from the fibromyalgia. To be sure there isn't anything else, I have to go and get some bloodwork done. Woo-hoo," she exclaimed without smiling. "I told him that if he wanted me to be in a room with a needle he was going to have to tranquilize me first. Oh man, I was crying practically the whole time I was in there, 'cause I really don't like doctors' offices, and he said I might want to see someone in mental health--like, because I'm upset, that means I'm crazy or something."

"Okay, so did he give you a number or anything?"

"No. I am not going to mental health. Like I said, it was horrible on the coast, and I even tried it out here in Salida a few months ago. It was a joke. You have to talk to this mental technician or whatever she's called for the first several visits. You don't get to see anyone who can actually help for a while. They make you fill out forms and take home a bunch of papers with drawings of different facial expressions, to help you identify your feelings. Seriously? Are we in kindergarten? I mean, come on, I know what I'm feeling. I just want to move on finally, and I don't know how. When I objected and told her that I wanted to speak to someone who could actually help me, she accused me of just wanting to see a doctor so I could get drugs prescribed. Fucking bitch, I told her that I had been through years of therapy and I wanted to talk to someone who would intuitively know how to help me, not some kid who had to look at the computer screen to know what to ask me next."

"Nice," she chuckled. "Although, they may be able to help you connect ..."

"I am not going to mental health!"

"Look, if you can't go to the store without having an anxiety attack or yelling at someone, and you're hearing motors in your head, it seems to me that those are signs that you need help. We'll find a good psychiatrist; I'll look in the phone book for you, alright?"

"I guess." Then she changed her mind and shook her head. "No, I need to see a psychologist, or a therapist or something; someone who won't try to talk me into taking drugs, or accuse me of trying to get them. I want someone who will actually help me for a change. I've been in therapy, on and off, for over twenty years--ever since the car accident. That's crazy! I want to actually fix the problem. Something has to change, but no good shrink is going to see me without insurance."

"I bet there's someone out there that will work with you."

That evening, after pacing back and forth in our tiny apartment for awhile, my lady got down on her knees next to the futon. I thought she might be looking for the toy I couldn't find earlier, but she began talking to the ceiling fan. She was crying as she angrily told it to bring her help; she told it that she didn't deserve to live like this and insisted that it take away the pain.

"You *help* me," she insisted as the tears streamed down her face. She put her head on the bed and cried for several minutes; then she raised her head, wiped her tears and her nose and said, "Thank you, Spirit."

For a while I had thought that, maybe, she was losing her sanity, but I have gotten used to her talking to various objects-- trees, ceilings, clouds. I'm not sure I understand it; however, I always sense that it makes her feel better.

She made phone calls to a few people and, a week later, we met the woman that was finally able to help my green-eyed lady. I heard her tell my human that payments were made on something called a "sliding scale" and since she had so little income, and had applied for disability, no payment was necessary. When she heard this, I sensed suspicion rather than relief or gratitude. And I could also sense a hint of that determination I felt as she was preparing for us to walk, back in 2003.

Her anxiety was intense as we were leaving for the first appointment, and I could hear her breathing speed up as we stepped out the front door. Then she spun around, pulled me back in, shut the door, and sat back down at the kitchen table. She took a couple of deep, slow breaths and rose to face the door. Then she sat back down.

"Fuck!" She slammed her fist on the table. Again, she took a breath, got up and quickly walked to the door; I stood at her side as she reached for the door knob and pulled the door open before she could stop herself again.

"I can do this," she said as she quickly scooted me out the door and locked it behind her. She stood there for a moment, grasping the wooden railing tightly and looking down at the mat, which had been turned around so that it would "welcome" her into the world as she exited her sanctuary.

"I can do this," she repeated as she let go and we walked slowly down the stairs to the courtyard. When we got to the bottom, she took a deep breath and let it out; then we walked the sixteen blocks to the therapist's office.

Leaving the apartment, or her "cave," as her friend from Denmark called it, took at least this much effort each time. Whether we were going to see the safe lady therapist, whether we were going to the post office or going to the library, it took the same amount of effort. Many times she couldn't get herself out to any place other than the therapist, which she did with stubborn determination, every single week for a year and a half.

"How about we start with you telling me what your life is like right now. What does your day look like," the therapist asked.

"Well, it probably sounds boring, but ..."

"Okay, wait. First of all, no judgements, just tell it," she said with a warm smile. My lady took a deep breath and continued.

"I usually get up between two and four, depending on what time I went to bed; I don't ever sleep more than three hours at a time.

I make some decaf coffee or tea and listen to the radio while I do crossword puzzles, or draw or something. Sometimes I go back to bed for a few more hours. If I have to, I get out and get my errands done as soon as places are open because they're less crowded then. As long as the weather's good and I don't hurt too much, I take Ebby over to the river each day. I'm usually in for the day by mid-afternoon. I don't like being out later in the day, and by that time I'm getting pretty tired. So I watch the DVDs I got from the library." She stopped and thought for a minute. "That's pretty much it."

"Do you have friends that you hang out with," asked the therapist.

"There's the woman downstairs. We get along pretty well and we seem to like the same things. She's like me; she doesn't like to go out, especially if there are crowds. And it's perfect, she can't take the stairs because she has COPD, so she never comes knocking on my door when I want to be alone. We usually hang out in the courtyard while Ebby and her dog, Choowii, play. Choowii is sweet, but he's basically a mop head that barks a lot."

"Any other friends or people you associate with?"

"Um, not really. People annoy me, usually. I've never been a good judge of charactor for some reason, and I'm laughably gullible at times. So I learned to just doubt everybody. It's much easier to just be by myself. I have these bouts of rage, too, and I don't want everyone in this town to hate me."

"When does the rage happen?"

"Oh, it's totally random. I could be in a perfectly good mood, then the woman in front of me at the store pulls out a bunch of coupons or someone's whistling or the clerk won't stop chatting with the person bagging or they're playing jazz. Jazz is like chaos in my head and I can't focus. I never know what will set me off." She began speaking faster and hadn't taken a breath.

"Okay, let's stop for a minute. Take a deep breath on a count of four. Good. Hold it for a count of two and let it out slowly. Again." Once my lady had calmed down, the therapist asked more questions.

"You say you feel anxiety, but not just about going out in public?"

"Mostly, but I have attacks when I'm not going anywhere, too. It's so noisy where I live. I mean, I expected loud music, but oh man, there are all kinds of trucks and motors, so many motors, and the kids ride their skateboards on the sidewalk right under my window."

"Can you explain what happens when you feel the anxiety?"

"Sometimes I forget to breath at all; sometimes I start breathing fast. I can feel this pressure in my chest. It feels like there's a fist in there wrapped around the base of my throat. I lose my balance; I start shaking and I feel irritable. Feels like I can't think clearly, like I can't think of the next thing to do."

"And you say that motors set you off?"

"Yeah. I think it's from the car accident in 1985. I was trapped in the car and it was on fire. My husband, at the time, burned his fingers trying to put my boots out; they had to use those jaws of life to get me out. Once, a shrink ... sorry, a doctor, told me that that was why certain engines set me off, because it was such a loud motor and it was right by me. But a kid on a skateboard can set me off just as bad."

"Anything else?"

"I don't know...feeling trapped ..."

"Okay, how do you feel here? Are you comfortable, or do you feel overwhelmed by the questions?"

"I feel okay here. And I'm okay with the questions," my lady answered, shifting in her seat. She had been sitting for a while now and was getting uncomfortable.

"I'm in a little pain from sitting still, but otherwise, I'm good," she paused and looked around. "Actually, this office feels good, comfortable."

"Good, I'm glad. This is a safe place. Just let me know if it gets too bad. And you can always get up and walk around if you like. Alright, can you tell me a little more about the car accident? What sort of injuries did you have?"

"It was in December of 1985. We were on our way to work, my husband and I, and there was about an inch of new snow on the ground. Some young guy coming the opposite way was driving too fast because he was late for work. He worked at the hospital, in Morristown, which we had just passed. The joke was that he was the only one who made it to work that day. Anyway, he got cut off and hit his brakes. He spun around a couple of times and landed in our lane.

"I wasn't wearing my seatbelt because I didn't want to wrinkle my blouse. Except for noticing how, with all the snow on the trees, it looked like a fairyland and that we had been listening to "Down on the Corner" on the radio, I don't remember anything. Whatever else I know about it is from what people told me. I tried to remember, with hypnosis, amitol, nothing worked."

"Okay, and the injuries," the therapist asked as she continued to write.

"My head hit the windshield, causing damage to the left frontal lobe and making my brain swell; I bit down on my tongue and caused nerve damage and broke two front teeth; I stuck out my left hand to brace myself and broke two fingers, and both legs snapped at the shins when I was forced under the dashboard. The left leg was broken in six places and the right in two. Also, my right foot was broken, but they missed it, just like they missed the fingers on my left hand. They had to take a graft from my hip a while later, and re-break my foot. Because my brain was swelling, they put me in a coma for about four days until the edema went down. I spent a month in the hospital, then a few months in a wheelchair."

"Wow, sounds like you've answered that question a few times," she laughed. "Just a few more for today, okay? What are the lasting symptoms from the accident?"

"I have short-term memory loss, PTSD and random aches and pains. And I have to really pay attention when someone is telling me something, especially if it's new instructions or something.

Otherwise, it just doesn't stay in there," she tapped the side of her head with her finger.

"What about medications? Do you take any?"

"I don't take anything now. They tried all kinds of things, but they always made me feel worse. They always made it harder to think, and ..." she paused.

"And what?"

"Well," I could feel her hesitation, and I sensed embarrassment. "I'd feel disconnected, like I couldn't get through to the Spirit, the Universe."

"That's a perfectly valid feeling. There's no reason for embarrassment. Please remember that this is a safe place, and there are no judgements, okay? And I want you to know that I feel it's good for you to have a source of power that isn't you, yourself."

"Oh no, you're not going to use that stuff from the *Big Book* are you? I am long past being able to be powerless; it helped me for a while, but then it wasn't enough anymore. I did that for fifteen years; then I re-read a book that my dad gave me a long time ago, *Science of Mind*. It's about the law of attraction and drawing on the energy that is everywhere. It's empowering because I know that I direct the energy. I pray for guidance and clarity; but, there's none of that Thy Will Be Done crap, thank you very much."

"If I may," she interrupted, "I am very familiar with the book and the law of attraction and I fully support it's use and agree with the principles."

"Okay. Really? ... Cool." My lady took a breath and continued, "Anyway, they tried nardil, prozac, xanax, neurontin, and effexor over the years. There were a couple of others, but I can't remember any more names right now."

They talked for almost an hour, then the therapist asked my green-eyed lady if she felt they were at a good stopping point, and if she felt comfortable leaving. When my human said she was good, she was handed a small card with the time and date of our next appointment. They shook hands, the therapist looked down at me and said goodbye, and we walked home.

"Well, that didn't hurt too much I suppose. She didn't tell me I need drugs, she didn't make me fill out a bunch of forms, and she didn't roll her eyes or go blank when I mentioned *Science of Mind*. I think I like her. What do you think?" I wagged my tail. She was smiling a little, and that made me happy.

****

CHAPTER ELEVEN

During the next two months, we had visited the lady therapist once or twice each week. For awhile my lady just needed to talk, to say all the things that had been in her head for so long. There were times when I could make no sense of what she said, she just cried a lot and spewed words and emotions, sometimes without even forming sentences. The therapist-lady sat and listened to everything, periodically taking notes, but mostly just listening.

My human was taught some breathing methods, to help her relax herself; and once she had given sufficient background information, the therapist felt comfortable beginning the actual treatment. It was called EMDR, which she said stood for Eye Movement Desensitization and Reprocessing.

"To put it simply, this will help you to process painful things that happened in the past, the way we do in dreams. Just like when you're in REM sleep, the mind and body are processing what has been experienced and then are able to release it. This process takes the charge, if you will, out of the negative memory. Then we replace the negative feeling with a positive one and reinforce it," the therapist explained.

They tried it for a few minutes and stopped; my lady said that moving her eyes back and forth like that was giving her a headache, so the therapist opened the desk drawer and removed a small black box with a couple of dials and lights on it. Attached to the box were two long wires, each with an oval piece of plastic at the end. My lady held one "buzzie," as the therapist called it, in each hand as the vibrations alternated from hand to hand.

"Okay, this is going to work on the same principle as the rapid eye movement; the left to right stimulation in your hands will act the same way. Let's see what settings are comfortable for you. We can control the speed and intensity; you just tell me when it feels right."

Once the dials were set, the therapist would ask if my lady was comfortable, suggesting she put her feet flat on the floor to feel more grounded, and then they began as I walked over and curled up under her desk. Sometimes, I didn't like accompanying her to therapy. Being so sensitive to her feelings, I was almost in pain as I felt the emotions, which seemed to surge from her and bounce around the room. There were times when her feelings were so intense that I could see the energy radiating all around her; it looked like the air over black pavement on a hot day, like on the day in Keyenta when she was chatting with those nice reservation policemen. On that day, even the human officer could feel her energy.

"What would you like to start with today? Do you want to go in and clear out any feelings about the accident," the therapist asked.

"I don't know," she shrugged her shoulders. "It really doesn't bother me any more; I mean I still have some triggers from it, but it doesn't seem like a big deal. I have no memory of the actual accident. I know I went through something horrible, because people told me all about it, but it's more like the memory of a movie."

"That's good! Would you like to talk about your ex-husband or your son today?"

"Nope."

"Okay, how about your trip to El Salvador? Do you feel comfortable talking about that?"

"I guess ... not sure what to say about it."

"Why don't you just start with telling me how the trip came about. Follow the train of thought and see if that brings anything up, okay? Then we can go in and clear out whatever holds a charge." The therapist picked up the pad and pen.

"Well, I had heard about the earthquakes down there--two major quakes, almost exactly one month apart. My husband talked a lot about Central America, Nicaragua and El Salvador mostly, and we were always listening to public radio. Like it or not, I was becoming more aware of stuff going on outside the U.S. and started getting the feeling like I wanted to do something, like I should get involved somehow.

"I called a few numbers that he suggested and told them that I'd like to help, thinking they'd just want me to raise money or something. It was a young guy that answered the phone, and he *challenged* me.

"'If you really want to help, you'll get on a plane and go down there with the next delegation. Then you can decide for yourself what you can do for them.'

"The idea was that we would be bringing earthquake relief to the people who supported the FMLN, that's the left wing. They used to be insurgents and were labeled as terrorists; however, now they are a legitimate political party. And they were elected into power in 2009. I love it when stuff like that happens.

"More importantly though, we'd be witnessing what was happening down there. Ideally we, the delegates, would then bring the information back to the states and talk about it. I figured this'd be good for me to do. And I think I wanted to see for myself. All my life I had been told that things were a certain way; now, I was being told that it was all a lie. Man, I had no idea! That trip changed everything. All those years I was raised to believe that we were the good guys, that America was the knight in shining armor, that we were always helping others and stopping crazy despots and keeping the peace." She paused as she remembered to breathe.

"I went down there, and I saw this country from the outside. I was overwhelmed, and I just didn't know what to do with all the information I was getting. We're *not* the good guys! All my life I believed the lie--all my life. How could I be so stupid? How could I be so completely ignorant and unquestioning? And how can they lie to us like that? I hate being lied to. I'm so gullible. Oh, it really pisses me off ..."

"Breathe," said the therapist, and my lady took a huge breath and let it out slowly. After a few moments she asked, "Where was I?"

"Well, I think you had decided to make the trip," the therapist said, then made a suggestion. "How about telling me what was going on in your life before you left."

"Okay so, we were living in a tent on some land about ten miles north of Ft. Bragg, right on the coast, "Land of the Misfits," I called it. What a bunch of whackos living there; but it was safe and offered a couple of months of stability while I hunted for a place to live, so I was pretty grateful they were there."

"I'm sorry," the therapist said. "I just want to clarify something. You mention Ft. Bragg. I thought that was in North Carolina."

"There's also one in California, about ten miles north of Mendocino. It's a harbor town, Noyo Harbor. It's pretty nice, but since they clear-cut most of the redwoods and caught so many fish, it's main business is tourism."

"Okay, I appologize for interrupting your train of thought but I was confused," she smiled.

"No worries. Although, now you have to remind me where I was again." It was her turn to smile. Once the lady therapist reminded her, my lady continued.

"My husband wouldn't work, and I hadn't been able to find any work, either. I couldn't find us a place to live. Our situation was draining me. I know now, having gone back and talked to people, that it didn't matter how much I tried, my husband's reputation preceded him, and no one was going to rent to us.

"Oh, I'm not exaggerating, he had made himself a little name when he was doing some activist work some years ago; he was on the radio and local television talking about a few different projects. Then he started drinking and was caught on camera a couple of times as he acted out. Honestly, people knew who he was. However, I was not a local, and I was not involved in the activist sector of our community yet, and I had heard nothing about him." She paused and rolled her eyes. "I got off track.

"Anyway, I started getting this feeling, like I needed to do something drastic to change our situation. Maybe I was flailing, but it felt important for me to take this trip. I don't know, sometimes I get an idea in my head, and it seems crazy even to me when I say it out loud. But I can see it happening. I know I'm going to do it and I become obsessed with it until it happens.

"I just couldn't sit still in our situation. I was raised in a nice little middle class suburb in New Jersey, my childhood life looked like the set of *Father Knows Best* or something. And I was such a little nerd--before it was cool," she laughed. "When I hitched out to California, in 1989, I didn't have a place for a while. But this was different. I couldn't see an end to this!

"I swear, it felt as if his energy was cancelling out mine, and he seemed to have no desire, whatsoever, to live differently. He was nothing like I thought he was when I fell in love. He was perfectly happy to live in poverty, and have me take care of us. How can anyone in that situation not be straining, every day, to improve? Anyway, I just kept trying different things to give us a jump start, or an energy shift or something. There had to be some way out. I didn't belong there. I mean, my son and I had had a nice little apartment on Walnut Street. We'd ride our bikes to his preschool each day, I'd drop him off, then I'd go to work at a bed and breakfast in town. We had a nice little life."

"Okay, so apparently there are a couple of charges there. If you're comfortable, let's keep going, though. Tell me more about the actual trip now, and once we have a more complete image we can go in and clear it out."

My lady nodded and continued.

"I had a month to get ready and raise money to bring to the earthquake victims. I had just gotten a tax refund so I bought a plane ticket and things I needed for the trip; there was still money left over for gas to get to the airport, and to take care of my family for the ten days I was gone.

"This was pre-September Eleven so I had no trouble getting an expedited passport, which took almost exactly a month, and picked it up on the way to the airport. It was crazy; they said I had to take a midnight flight, so that I'd arrive in the morning, after sunrise. They said the road to the airport was too dangerous in the dark. I was told to 'bring cash--small bills.' The money was going directly to the people, not through some government agency. Since it was to help communities that supported the FMLN (Farabundo Marti Liberacion Nacional), the right wing government would intercept it.

"And what did your husband think about all this?"

"He was practically pushing me to do this. He never actually did anything to help, but he was verbally supportive. He's the one who suggested I make the phone calls. But," she hesitated and frowned. "I don't even know how he actually felt any more. We were together for over six years and I feel like I never even knew him. Now it feels like everything he said was a lie, like he was putting me on the whole time." My lady paused and shook her head before continuing.

"I had heard that term before, you know, 'gaslighting.' But I never knew what it meant until I watched that movie on DVD last year. I couldn't believe it when I saw it; I just sat there crying. That's what he did! He knew I had trouble with my memory, so he'd "remind" me of things. He'd make up stories, but he inserted just enough truth in them to always keep me doubting myself. I had no idea who or what to trust. Do you know that, toward the end of the marriage, he even tried to convince me that he was working with my dad to have me put away?

"When we met he was on parole, having been in prison for what he did to an ex-girlfriend. He had kicked in her door and attacked her and her new boyfriend. Of course, that's not what he told me; he said he was framed and he had to make some kind of deal, because he was growing weed. He was such a liar; I don't get how I didn't see through it.

"He had been staying with my best friend, who lived in the same apartment complex as my son and me. We had all had dinner together one night. After that I didn't see him again, or even wonder why I didn't see him, for about a year because he was back in prison. Then I saw him at a twelve-step meeting and I was just needing a distraction." She paused and grinned.

"The sex was okay and I was done, not wanting anything more from him. He left flowers at my door the next morning. He was intense, and I guess I was needing that kind of attention. For a while he treated me like a goddess; he actually looked at me like he thought I was beautiful.

"When we were together for a month or so he got drunk, took my truck and caused a hit and run accident. I had to go down to Mendocino with another friend to find him and my truck, and drive them back. When we got home, he pushed me around for a bit when I wouldn't give him any money. My son was at his dad's; I went down and locked myself in my pick-up until he passed out. By the time this all happened it was too late for me to just turn it off, or walk away; I was completely under some crazy spell, totally insane. I mean, what was I thinking? He really was a dirt bag.

"He went back to prison for another seven months, because he violated his parole by drinking and driving. And I drove to the bay area to see him every single week because I felt so bad for him being in there. Then, after seven months in prison he got out, got drunk, and hit me again. I called the cops this time because my son was hiding behind the couch and crying as he banged on the apartment door for me to let him in; he wound up back in there for a forty-five-day dry out. So what do I do? When he gets out the second time I marry him in a courthouse on the way home from the prison. Haha, that'll teach him, huh?

"The thing was, he taught me so much, truly opened up my world. I started seeing everything with a different perspective. If it wasn't for him I never would have gone to El Salvador, and I never would have done all that walking. I never would have gone to all those music festivals and rallies--there's so much I would not be aware of, so many experiences I wouldn't have had. He was my Eskimo. And the thing is, he'd seem totally supportive. He encouraged me to do things. Then he would somehow sabotage what ever I did. I don't get it. I can't tell you how many things he ruined for us," she stopped, frowned and squinted her eyes at the therapist.

"I didn't want to talk about him. You tricked me."

"What?" She smiled innocently.

I couldn't help it, I chuckled; but it came out as a snort, which made them both look at me, then at eachother, then break into laughter--which sliced through the tension in the small room. Once they recovered, my lady continued talking about the trip.

"I had never seen, nor did I imagine there could be, so many shades of green. It was so gorgeous as we flew over the jungle and into San Salvador. Getting off the plane you're blasted with hot air. Buildings are all open, there is no air conditioning in most places. In the airport you have to wait in line, and one by one you step up. Red or green lights flash to tell you whether you can go through, or whether you have to be searched. It flashed green for me so I was able to proceed without being mauled by security.

"The group leader was late arriving at the airport, but just when I started to get concerned she showed up with a flirty taxi driver and they took me to a safe house. She said if I ever got separated and needed help I should call him and he would get me to safety, and he passed his card back to me.

"I loved the house. It had concrete walls that stopped a foot short of the roof, so it was all open. A large dark green metal wall covered the front of the house; there was a door in the metal wall which, in turn, had a small metal door at eye level so you could give a password and they could see you before they opened the door. No kidding, it was just like in a movie. There was no hot water, but it was so hot there that the icy, spring fed, showers were a blessing. I liked the Salvadoran food. I was surprised, it wasn't very spicy. They had this cheese that looked kind of like mozzarella, but it was dry and salty. Oh, and the pupusas were amazing." She grinned and stopped when she noticed the therapist smiling because she had gotten off track.

"I fell a little bit in love with the people. They were so warm and friendly, and they looked me in the eye when they spoke to me. When they asked 'how are you' it seemed like they actually wanted to know, not like here. And from what I saw in the brief time I was there, they were so strong; they had been through such heartwrenching things ..." her eyes filled with water and she blinked it away.

"The first night, we watched a movie called "Maria" about a woman, and her family, that fought in the war. She was just a regular woman--a mom, a wife. Then she and her husband had no choice but to pick up guns and fight; they were in separate units, so sometimes they'd go a year without seeing each other or knowing if the other was alive. She had to be separated from her children, too. One night, as her unit was camping in the jungle, they heard the screams of a woman being tortured and killed. The next day as they broke camp they came across the body of the young woman who had died, and it was her daughter. I was bawling from then on. During the trip I cried every day, at least once. I couldn't help the tears streaming down my face as I listened to these people.

"We went to the UCA, the University of Central America, in San Salvador and listened to a beautiful lady, a professor, speak about the Jesuit priests--her friends--that were killed there. The priests were in the living quarters; the groundskeeper was off working and his wife, the housekeeper, and their sixteen-year-old daughter were in their room. SOA trained paramilitary came in and dragged the priests out into the courtyard. They were teaching Liberation Theology. They were teaching people to think, to know that no one is better than anyone else, and their heads ..." she stopped and cleared her throat. Her voice was strained as she continued. "Their heads were symbolically destroyed; they showed us the pictures--one of those things I wish I could unsee. A rose bush was planted in the spot where each priest fell.

"The housekeeper and her daughter were hiding in their room when the paramilitary did a sweep to be sure there were no witnesses, because the intention was to blame the FMLN. The professor said that they must have heard the women crying and went in and shot them." She stopped for a moment to blow her nose.

"This professsor was friends with the priests and the family, so they blew up her house and she had to go into hiding.

"This is not a new story, but it was all new to me. Before I met my ex, I rarely listened to the news, and when I got a newspaper it was so I could do the crossword puzzle. When I did listen, I'd hear stuff like this, but it never resonated. I never actually felt it. I'd shake my head and think, 'oh those poor people,' then go about my day. But being there, right where it happened, talking to the people who went through it--feeling the energy--I didn't know what to do with it. Those paramilitary were trained in our country! They were trained right there in Ft. Benning, Georgia. Our tax money goes to places like that!" She was unable to force any more words out. Her tear drenched face was getting red.

"Okay, you need to breathe," she said and paused while my lady took a few paced breaths. "Why don't we take a break for a few minutes. Maybe step outside or splash water on your face," the nice therapist said.

"No, I'm good. Can we keep going," my lady asked after she blew her nose.

"Sure, if you're comfortable."

"Look, before we go any farther, I realize I don't have to, but I feel the need to tell you I'm not one of those people that hates our country or anything. I love this country! And I'm so grateful that this is my home. That being said, I most definitely am afraid, and have much mistrust, of the dozen or so rich guys running everything. Their lack of concern for anyone or anything outside their circle is frightening and eggregous.

"When I was in El Salvador, and when I was walking, I heard pretty much the same thing from so many people. The people in El Salvador said that they didn't hate Americans; they hated what our government was doing to them. And they understood the dynamics; where they live there are seven families that run the country. They were amused by how we are so efficiently controlled by our media. Also, here in the states, no one said they hated this country, not one person. But they were all pretty upset about how things are being run and what the people in charge have been doing in their names.

"You're right, you didn't need to say that; however, I appreciate that you did. You okay to continue?"

"Uh-huh.

"For ten days we learned about some pretty heavy shit; every day we were exposed to a new horror. One night, we met with the FARC from Columbia. That night was like something out of an old novel or movie. It felt like it should have been in black and white, you know? It was toward the end of the trip and I had been overwhelmed with information and emotions and I was feeling a little loopy, I think. The whole scene seemed so surreal.

"The meeting took place at the safe house, the roof was corrugated tin and mangos kept falling from the trees, making everyone jump and laugh nervously each time they hit the roof with a loud bang. There was a storm, complete with heavy rain, thunder and lightening, just like there was at this time every day. It was like they scheduled the meeting at that time for the effect.

"We sat in a meeting room, which was lined with frowning men holding very large guns, and listened to a few men at a table at one end of the room tell about such horrible things--la corbata, la camiseta--and all kinds of horrible ways of killing and torturing people. It was like they were bragging, like they were there for the shock value. I didn't like them very much, and I wasn't really impressed with them like I was supposed to be. This was supposed to be one of the highlights of the trip, 'appearing for one night only.' We had been instructed not to mention their arrival to anyone until after it was confirmed that they had safely left the country after the meeting. Frankly, I was much more impressed with the women that ran the coffee cooperative, and the people of Nejapa. Maybe they started out the same but, the FARC seemed very different from the FMLN.

"Actually, I was more concerned about the bugs, than with what the FARC had to say. As we sat listening to them, a huge green bug landed on the shoulder of the young man sitting in front of me. I didn't want to disturb him, but I couldn't just let it sit there, so I knocked it off and it hit the floor. Then I couldn't see it so I pulled my feet up off the floor as I looked around for it. I wasn't aware that anyone was looking at me until I heard a soft chuckle. I turned to see one of those guys with the big guns looking at me and trying to stifle his laughter."

My green-eyed lady had gotten off track again, but she had become animated and there was a sparkle that I rarely saw anymore in her eyes. I think that's why the lady therapist let her continue.

"At one point, we spent a night out in the campesinos; there was an organic coffee cooperative in the jungle, run completely by women. It was about an hour drive outside of the city on a dirt road. And make no mistake, we were in the real live jungle. The bus pulled to the side of the road, the doors opened and we filed out. I looked around and only saw dense greenery. There was nothing, until we walked through a small opening in the trees and took a path to what looked like a campground of sorts. There were a few small huts and an open, but covered, meeting area with tables, chairs and hammocks. Just past that was a communal cooking area, in the center of which was a large steaming pot sitting on an open fire. Children giggled and ran around playing with little dogs. These dogs all looked like they came from the same litter. All shades of tan and white, and they all had huge deer-ears that stood straight up. They weren't named; they weren't pets like here, they were all just called 'aguacatitos' because they lived off the avocados that fell from the trees.

"That night, every family from the campesino contributed something and we were made the most delicious meal I had on the entire trip. One of the women stayed up all night sewing small bags so she could give all fifteen of us coffee to take home. The people were all so beautiful. Being with them felt good. I wanted to hug them all.

"I thoroughly enjoyed this part of the trip, until we had to spend the night outside. The Jesus Bus (pronounced heysoos-boos) drivers took us to another part of the compound, a fenced in area with an unused building. As we set up our pads to sleep on the concrete porch of this building I started seeing the bugs.

"One guy goes, 'don't worry, when the lights go out they will go away.'

"I said, 'yeah, nice try.'

"Sitting on the wall of the porch and my legs started shaking; I couldn't think very clearly and I was on the verge of tears. The pressure in my chest was making it difficult to breathe.

"'I want to sleep in the Jesus Bus,' I told the leader of our group. She told me that that wasn't going to happen. The drivers were in there and it wouldn't be appropriate. I told her that I wasn't concerned with what was appropriate, that I was not going to be able to sleep with all these bugs and other things crawling around. I said I just couldn't do it.

"One of the guys in our delegation had brought himself some netting for the occasion. I don't know if he volunteered, or if he was coerced, but he handed it over for the sake of calming me down. It was attached to the wall and came down and was tucked in all around my padding like a little tent. The others stayed up drinking (and probably laughing at me) but I had had enough, so I put in my earplugs and let them wrap the netting around me and I slept deeply until morning.

The next day, I was talking with one of our translators who lived in San Salvador. He said he got me a joint because he saw how overwhelmed I was. That evening, he drove me to his house so I could smoke comfortably. He said he wasn't able to drive me back, but the Jesus Bus drivers were going to stop by to get me. We sat out on a patio in his stone-fenced yard. For the first time since I had been there, I looked up at the sky; the stars were magnificent. I felt like I could relax for a few moments. It was just the break I needed.

"A while later, as we were driving back to the safehouse, I realized that it was taking much longer to get back than it had taken to get to the translator's house. I was sitting a few seats from the front in this, otherwise, empty bus. My heart started to pound. I could feel it in my ears, and I could feel that fist clenching my throat. Those guys seemed nice, but what did I know? I just sat there in the bus thinking about how people disappeared, how people were killed--in such brutal ways--and I didn't really know these guys at all. I couldn't believe I had been so careless. One of the guys glanced back to look at me. I've been told that my face is an open book; I guess it's true, because his eyes got wide and he held up his hands trying to calm me, although, I had not said a word.

"'Esta bien! Esta bien! Estas a salve!' He explained that I was safe, that there was road work being done, and several one way streets, so we had to take a detour. He kept turning around and smiling at each turn to reassure me that we were almost there, 'Sin peligro. Casi alli. Esta bien. Casi alli.'

"I didn't unclench my fists, even though I had actually drawn blood in my palms, until we arrived at the safehouse. This was another of the many times I have said, 'Wow, that could've sucked. Thank you, Spirit.'

"Other than that, it was meetings and lectures. We met with unions and the nurses from STISS, which is their social services. We went to maquilas; although, we weren't actually allowed to go into the Free Trade Zone, or even slow down (which speaks volumes to whether it's a good thing or not) so we took pictures as we drove by. We met with several people from the FMLN ..." she paused.

"Oh! We took turns, and each day one person from the delegation got to give the 'salud,' which is the formal welcome, in spanish, to the person or people we were meeting. You had to write something up yourself. When it was my turn I got to give the salud to the woman who was the Senator and second in command of the FMLN. I don't know if it meant anything to anyone else, but I was pretty stoked.

"The FMLN representatives took us to several towns that had been devastated by the earthquakes, like Las Colinas where there was a landslide because they had cut down a bunch of trees on a hill so rich people could build their homes up there. Down below, less than a week prior, people were protesting the clear-cutting for fear of a landslide that would bury all their homes, and that's just what it did. So many families were needlessly destroyed that day.

"We went to an FMLN governed town called Nejapa, where they had closed the cop shop and turned it into a library. It was so cool! And they had *Fireball* games every year, there. They'd wrap rags in wire, then let the balls soak in gasoline. Then, they'd put on extra layers of clothing and gloves, and they'd light the balls and throw them at each other!

"Some places were so awesome; other's made me cry. We visited refugee camps, where there were so many children! And they were living on rationed food and water, in small corregated metal sheds. On the way to Nejapa there were vast garbage dumps; the smell was so bad we had to close all the windows of the bus and pull our shirts up over our noses. As we slowed, we saw that there were people actually living right there in the dumps. I couldn't bring myself to take any pictures, it just seemed disrespectful. They made their homes out of whatever they could find there. The people were called 'buitres,' vultures, by the local people. It was awful.

"On the flight home I sat in a stupor, amongst a gaggle of sunburned tourists cackling away about their vacations. It didn't seem that we had all just come from the same country.

"'Wasn't it beautiful? Oh, the beaches are fantastic! The nightclubs! The food! They treat you like gods down here, and everything's so cheap. I love throwing coins on the ground and watching all the kids scramble after them.'

"Okay, I have to ask, 'Jesus Bus'?" She pronounced it with long U's at the end of each word like my lady did.

"Yeah," she laughed, "that was our cover. We drove around in this big bus with a mural of Jesus on it."

****

CHAPTER TWELVE

"If at any time you feel that this is too much, I want you to tell me. We will stop, breathe through it, and talk if you want," said the therapist. She and my lady had been working intensely with the buzzies.

Whenever they used them, I could feel the release of energy into the room. When we'd leave and she'd just breathe and walk quietly back to our home on Sackett. Sometimes, we'd go straight to the river and I'd dive for rocks for a few minutes before we'd go back to the apartment. Without fail, the next morning she'd be exhausted and kind of cranky when I woke her to let me outside. But by mid-day the mood would pass. With each of those cycles, the result was better than the time before. Each time I felt her get lighter, happier and healthier, and the festering odor diminished with each session.

Today they were going to begin to process her feelings about her son. Last week my lady had finally begun to talk about how guilty she felt for letting him down. She had told the therapist that she felt a physical pain, and constriction, in her chest and throat when she thought about the situation they were in a few years ago.

"When I was pregnant with him, I kept thanking the Spirit for letting me take care of him. I was so grateful to be his mom. I felt that it had to be a miracle; his father and I were more buddies than lovers. Sex didn't happen very often; we mostly played and had fun together. Haha, we even went to an amusement park for a week on our honeymoon. It wasn't like it was a bad thing; we enjoyed each other and it worked.

"My son was such an easy baby. He was sleeping through the night within a few weeks of being born. He was happy, beautiful, smart, and very aware. I never did that 'baby talk' with him, none of that googoo-gaga crap and no cutsie names for things. I spoke to him as I would an adult, and people always commented on his vocabulary. One time, we were walking along the bluffs on the coast and some guy was getting a toy rocket ready to shoot in the air for his kids. We paused, and he told my son to watch. It shot into the air and burst into confettti; all his kids squealed with delight.

"My son says, 'But what about all the debris?' He was about six at the time.

"There was no physical discipline. I had gotten smacked a few times when I was a kid, but mostly I'd get grounded or lose tv or something. So I wasn't raised with that 'spare the rod' mentality, thank goodness. When he was young I swatted him on two occasions. It wasn't hard but it was enough to make me feel sick inside. I don't even remember what had happened, but I remember that I felt it was my responsibility, like I was supposed to, but it felt so horrible. I never did it again. I can still feel a twinge when the image comes. I can still see the hurt in his eyes, like he couldn't understand how I could do that to him.

"In the eleven years that we were together, he didn't get in trouble in school at all. The worst thing that ever happened was when his teacher approached me when I was picking him up after classes one day, because she was frustrated.

"'Your son has trouble sitting still sometimes. I'll be in the middle of teaching a lesson, with all the students quietly listening. Out of nowhere he gets up, does a little dance in the aisle, and then returns to his seat as if nothing happened. Completely disrupts my class.' She couldn't help chuckling.

"I absolutely loved being his mom. I mean that. He was a great kid, very happy and easy going. And he was funny; he had a great sense of humor right from the get-go.

One day he was sitting at the kitchen table and said, 'Excuse me.'

"I asked, 'What for? I didn't hear you burp.'"

"'It was a diaper burp,' he laughed.

"We were together all the time, no babysitters. I didn't work very much for the first couple of years of his life, then I worked when he was in preschool. With him, I felt pure joy. When I was around him I just wanted to smile. I like that feeling--haven't felt it for a long time. And I was surprised at my feelings. I was never the nurturing, motherly type; always thought I was too selfish to be a good mom. I've always been one of those 'brush-yourself-off-and-get-over-it' kind of people; I had a no-nonsense mom, and that's how I was raised. A few weeks before my baby was conceived, I remember talking with some friends, about the fact that, at twenty-nine, I still hadn't had kids.

"'I always thought you were supposed to have kids before you turned thirty; it's just what I always had in my head. Works for me. I don't even like kids anyway.'

"I conceived a week later, and had my son less than one month before my thirtieth birthday.

"One thing I insisted upon was honesty between us. I told him, 'I'll stand behind you 100%, no matter what, but that means I have to know that I can trust your word. So we need to never lie to each other. If you lie once, I will always wonder.' As far as I know, he has never lied to me.

"When he was about ten, his best friend's mother knocked on the front door. She was angry and accused my son of stealing some game cards from her kitchen drawer.

"'He was the only one in there besides me and my son. I know it had to be him.'

"I called him out of his bedroom. 'Look me in the eye. Did you take the cards?'

"'No.' When I raised my eyebrow and looked at him hard he added, 'I didn't, Mom!'

"'He says he didn't. Something else must have happened to them.'

"'That's it? You're not even going to investigate or punish him or anything?'

"'Punish him? For what? My son is not a thief; and he says he didn't take them. How should I investigate, anyway? Do you have a fingerprint kit or something?'

"With that she stormed out of the house, informing me that my son was no longer welcome in the house of his best friend. His other friends' mom said the same thing. My son 'could not be trusted and he wasn't welcome' in her home either.

"This was when I was getting ready to walk. His other friend's mom actually yelled at me when I went over to talk to her. She told me that I was a horrible mother and obviously didn't know what I was doing. Clearly I had no idea how to raise a child. Can you believe that she actually chastized me for not beating my son? 'You need to apply the belt on a regular basis.' She said that!

"The following week, that woman's youngest son fessed up when his older brother found the cards in his room. He said that, when the boys were playing out front and the other mom was in the shower, he went in the back door and took the cards from the kitchen drawer. His best friend's mom eventually apologized and we're good. But that other one never said a word."

Suddenly my lady's face got red and the tears flowed steadily down her cheeks. The lady therapist quickly pulled a few tissues from a box and handed them to her.

"I used to protect him--like when I went to his school because his second grade teacher had grabbed his arm and shoved him into his seat when he wasn't paying attention. I went in and gave them bloody hell, 'don't *ever* touch my son!' Once, I took him to the dentist and stood at his feet so we could keep eye contact while she drilled. I made her stop when his eyes welled up with tears. She hadn't given him enough novacaine although she insisted he was fine. I refused to let her continue until she gave him more. And... that's what a mom is supposed to do, right?

"My point is, we had a connection and a solid, healthy mother-son relationship. And he used to know that I would always protect him, that I would be right there by his side and never let anyone hurt him. But I let him down when he needed to know that I would keep him safe--and sheltered. That was my responsibility! I promised the Universe I would take care of him. I let him down and I don't even get why. My son had to be homeless for months! How is that fair to him? I let him down and all I can see is that beautiful face.

"Did your ex-husband beat your son?"

"No. But sometimes he'd just do something out of the blue. Once we were all sitting around the kitchen table. We were laughing and having a good time. It was warm and my son had no shirt on. All of the sudden, my ex hauls off and 'jokingly' slaps my little boy on the chest. We all just froze. My son tried to be stoic, but the tears came to his huge blue eyes and silently fell down to his chin and dropped to the red hand print on his chest. I just sat and looked at my husband and mouthed, 'what is *wrong* with you?' But that was it. Why didn't I get up and deck him? Why didn't I threaten him if he ever touched that little boy again? Another time, my son was refusing to eat his dinner. Frankly I didn't blame him. My husband wasn't a very good cook, but that was pretty much all he was willing to do. He started shoving forkfulls into my son's mouth, only stopping when he began to choke. Again, same thing, I did nothing. I just sat there crying with my son. *Why?* I love him so much," she paused for a second to breathe, but did not give the therapist time to answer.

"Then I go and leave for six weeks! I mean, he had other people. He wasn't alone with my ex all the time. There was his best friend; he'd spend the night there fairly regularly. And he went and stayed with his dad a couple of times, too. But I was his *mom.* We were always together. I was the constant in his life; I was the one he looked to for everything. We would talk on the phone, at least twice a week when I was away. I didn't know what was going on because he told me nothing. I know now that he couldn't. Shouldn't my Mother's Instinct have kicked in or something? I don't know why, but I truly thought that my husband would take responsibility if I wasn't around. We should have had a code word that my son could say so I would know to come right home ... or, I should have had him stay with his father. It just didn't occur to me."

At the end of that session, the therapist felt it was important for my lady to think of something positive about herself. After clearly struggling for a few moments, my lady shook her head.

"I'm sorry. I have nothing."

"Okay," the therapist paused, then asked, "How about when you were homeless, you were much more vulnerable, so you must have kept him safe, right? For instance, what were your sleeping arrangements?"

"When we were in the tent, I slept between him and my husband. My son was always right next to me so I could reach out in the dark and know he was okay," she paused and smiled weakly.

"Reminds me of the time we went on a weekend camping retreat with some friends. It was just the two of us in a large, screened cabin. We had a good time; but at night it was very dark in the woods and I have to admit I was almost as scared as he was. So we pulled the cots together and held hands and talked in the dark until we fell asleep."

"What I see," said the therapist, "is that you have made a few questionable choices; however, you did the very best that you could with the strength and information you had at the time--and, clearly, you did protect your son whenever it was possible for you to do so. It is important for you to take responsibility for your choices--but, try to go a little easier on yourself; seeing someone you love hurt another person you love makes for a very confusing situation. On top of that, your own safety was not assured. The couple of occasions, in which you say you froze, are completely natural. I am in no way saying the situation was not an awful one but, it appears to me that when your husband acted out, your son was never actually in danger. Knowing what I know about you, I am confident that you would have been able to intervene if he was.

"You deserve to be treated with the same loving compassion you give to your son. Do you hate him or ridicule him when he makes mistakes?"

"Of course not."

"Then use that as a guideline for self-talk and nurturing. If you wouldn't say it to your son, don't say it to yourself. I encourage you to go home and look in the mirror. Make eye contact. Then speak as you would if you were looking in your son's eyes. You deserve love and forgiveness from yourself."

This week she was actually sitting with the buzzies and clearing out the feelings, which meant she had to, repeatedly, relive the situations.

Her eyes were closed and she sat straight up in the chair, with her feet flat on the floor. In her hands the buzzies alternately vibrated, left to right. The therapist had instructed her to focus on an image, something with a heavy charge, in other words something painful, and just keep thinking about it. She was told to allow her mind to follow the train of thought from that point.

Her breathing became irregular; then she held it for the longest time as the tears flowed down her reddening face. I was just about to get up and put my head in her lap when the therapist spoke.

"Okay, breathe," the therapist said as she stopped the pulsing for a moment. Can you tell me what you were thinking?"

"I was picturing us at the kitchen table. I could see his eyes welling up with tears and the red hand on his white chest. Then I could see him hiding behind the couch while my husband was banging on the door to get in, he was praying, 'Please make him go away. Please make him go away.'" She was sobbing now.

"Let's go back in. Go to that original image again and see where it leads this time."

My lady closed her eyes again; her face and the front of her shirt were soaked with tears. Her feet squirmed furiously as though she was struggling to release them from bonds. As instructed, she brought up images of her son--over and over. They'd stop and she'd tell the therapist what new painful image had popped in to her head. Then she'd go back in and start again until the charge had decreased. Every so often the charge's intensity was measured by my lady, on a scale of one to ten. Once an image's charge got down to two or three, they moved on to another image.

The treatment continued for a full hour. This time, when we went home, my lady went straight to bed. She got up to feed and let me out and then immediately returned to the futon and pulled the covers up tight under her chin although it was a warm day. She didn't sleep. She just lay there staring as tears dripped silently from her eyes and soaked the pillow.

It took a few days for her to bounce back from that session. However, it was worth the wait to see her shine. For the first time since I've known my lady--she woke up grinning.

The following session was much more pleasant.

"Let's take some time this session to talk about happy memories. We'll do the same as we did when clearing things out; however, this will reinforce a positive flow of energy."

"So just randomly name happy memories?"

"Yeah," she smiled. "Start off with your Happy Place. Where do you go to calm yourself and attain clarity?"

"I used to go behind the house at Raven's Fall, where my son lives with his dad now; there was a log I'd sit on, and watch and listen to the water fall. It was very peaceful and private, very lush and green. I can still see it sometimes. Now I go to the river with Ebby. Just sitting there and watching her pick out rocks and put them on the shore is relaxing. The sound of the water flowing over the rocks is very soothing. That dog can almost always get me to grin. She has healing energy or something. All I know is I find myself grinning in spite of myself.

"Okay so that's a good one, 'Ebby at the river.' What else makes you grin? Just give me a list and I'll write them down so you have them when you need them."

"Drum circles! I get caught up in the rythmn and feel like I can not contain the joy. One year we went to Earthdance, out at the Black Oak Ranch in Northern California. My son was with his dad so it was just my husband and me. The festival organizers were attempting to make the world's largest drum circle, for the *Guiness Book of Records*. One of the drummers from the Grateful Dead was the conductor. He was on a platform, surrounded by the crowd. They handed out tamborine-styled drums to people that did not bring their own instruments. My husband had his own, so they gave me one. As we sat there, the famous drummer would point to different sections and we would play what he had taught us a few minutes prior. I could feel the waves pulsing through my body as I pounded on my drum. It was a moment of pure joy--pure connection. Very intense.

"A small plane flew overhead to photograph the entire circle. Rumors said that the pilot reported being able to feel the vibrations as he flew over us. Oh! And we did make it into the book of records. I keep my drum hanging on my wall."

"That sounds wonderful."

"We used to have fun when my son was little. We played a lot of games. He liked playing Pog when he was about three years old. It was a game where you each had a bunch of small cardboard discs, the size of a half dollar I guess. And you would hit them with a larger, heavier, disc called a Slammer. The idea was to get them to flip over and reveal pictures. Well, he would just reach down and turn a bunch over by hand if the disc didn't do the job.

I laughed and told him that was cheating.

"He says, 'I cheat. I win.'"

"When his dad had a caretaking job out at the Mendocino Woodlands, we lived out there in a nice little house. It was gorgeous--totally surrounded by redwoods--and there was a river and everything. My son was about two. We'd walk around and explore the woods and play at the river. It was one of the favorite times of my life; it was the lifestyle I always wanted. Seriously, wandering around in the redwoods, exploring and playing with my little son--how could it get any better than that?

"When we lived in town, and I didn't have a vehicle, we'd ride our bikes all over. He started riding a two-wheel--without training wheels--when he was about two and a half. It was amazing, one day he complained about them getting in the way and asked us to take them off. And that was it! When he was three or four we'd ride over to the preschool he attended when I was working at the bed and breakfast in town. People would beep and be laughing as they waved at us. He was so little! He had this miniature two-wheeler and this huge helmet.

"I remember riding one day, he was four I guess. He was, as usual, asking questions.

"'Mom, how come they say, 'stick and stones will break your bones, but words will never hurt you?' That's not true, because words really do hurt.'"

"'You're right, and sometimes they can hurt more, huh?'

"'Yeah,' he mused."

My lady paused for a moment as she seemed to be searching for more memories. I noticed that most of them had to do with her son, and then she dug deeper.

"When I was a kid we went to amusement parks pretty regularly." She grinned. "My dad and I would ride the roller coaster, get off, run around to the entrance and ride again.

"Hmm, what else? Oh! A couple of months before Ebby and I walked, I chaperoned an overnight field trip with my son's class to Angel Island, in the San Francisco Bay. We had fun. We all (parents, teachers and kids) dressed up in blue clothing. Then they put red tape down the sides of our pants and on our arms as rank stripes. We learned morse code and flag signalling; they even shot off a cannon. On the ferry back I opened a package of crackers and began to hold them in the air to feed the sea gulls that were following in our wake. The kids were loving it; all wanting a cracker to hold, and all screaming and giggling when a seagull would swoop in and grab one from their fingers.

"One of my favorite memories is Mother's Day in Pagosa Springs. My son had come out to stay with me for a few months, when I was renting the room from the man with cancer. There was an intense thunder and lightening storm happening, but it wasn't raining. We went out to the front lawn and lay on our backs and watched the brilliant show.

"'Happy Mother's Day,'" he laughed as we were laying there.

"Oh, good work; this is some great stuff. These are powerful, positive things to draw on."

****

CHAPTER THIRTEEN

"Okay, so remember I worked at the pancake place? There was this dishwasher working there; he seemed pretty nice, I guess. He came over once to help me move some furniture after work and he was always really nice to Ebony when I used to bring her to work. He said he learned how to be a dog trainer in prison. I know, right?" she added when her friend rolled her eyes.

"Anyway, once I quit working there I never saw him again, until the day before yesterday. He knocked on my door and said he hadn't been around because he'd been in jail for the past couple of years; and he said he'd been thinking about me the whole time."

"What?" Choowii's human laughed incredulously.

"Oh, wait. It gets way better. My gut said not to let him in and this time I actually listened. I told him I was pretty busy so I couldn't hang out. So he said he'd come back later on, even though I kept saying I was busy." She stopped to light a cigarette and took a deep drag.

The two women were drinking coffee at the picnic table in the courtyard while Choowii and I ran around the yard chasing my ball. He was small, young and quick, but he still could never get to the ball before me. I'd bring it to my lady, while he'd run behind me barking, "Give it to me! Throw it to me! Let me get it!" She'd absently throw it while she talked and laughed with her friend.

There had been a lot more laughter lately. My lady and I had been visiting the therapist for over a year now. And it seemed that, with every session with the therapist, that festering smell dissapated slightly; each week she seemed to brighten up a bit or something. The physical weight that she had been carrying for the past couple of years started to melt away, too, as she seemed to be eating differently and we were taking more walks. She was starting to smell like the lady I met all those years ago, but she smelled even better because she wasn't sad and frustrated like she used to be.

"It felt kind of weird that he showed up like that, so I told a couple of the guys upstairs to keep an eye out, because he wasn't invited. So yesterday morning the blond guy, you know from that apartment," my human pointed to his door on the second floor, "knocked on my door and said that my dishwasher-friend just robbed a bank. He also told me that the guy had come back and knocked on my door a few times yesterday, then he sat out in the courtyard for awhile and waited for me to come home before giving up and leaving.

"'So don't open your door because they haven't caught him yet.' I just laughed at him and went back inside to listen to the radio; then this morning I saw the paper. Can you believe this?" She opened the Salida newspaper that she had been holding.

"Oh my god, this isn't a joke," said Choowii's human. "It says he walked into the bank with a gun, wearing a baseball cap. He eluded the cops for a few hours, then they found him up on S Mountain." She shook her head.

"On the radio this morning they said that when they cornered him he threw all the money up in the air and laughed. Poor guy, sounds like he really just wanted to be back in prison," my lady added.

"Excuse me? 'Poor guy?' Seriously? How do you meet these people, anyway?"

"Well, I feel bad for him; whatever his motives, he was always nice to me, and it sounds like he spent so much time in there that he just wasn't comfortable outside anymore. And I don't know why I meet these people! It's like I'm some kind of Whacko Magnet or something. You wonder why I stay inside? People be crazy." She laughed and then frowned a bit.

"I don't get it. I mean, we keep getting the same lessons in life until we learn whatever we're supposed to learn, right? So what am I supposed to get from this? Don't trust anyone? Ever? Don't even *talk* to men? I've been celibate for years, so it's not like there's romantic interest or anything for me. Seriously, what am I supposed to be seeing?"

"I don't know. You're a strange one, neighbor-of-mine," her friend said as she rolled her eyes and laughed. My human threw the ball for me and, once again, Choowii didn't stand a chance.

"I'm so gonna write a book. This stuff is great. I don't even need an imagination; all I have to do is tell it like it happened. Haha, I could call it, 'I See Strange People.'"

While in therapy, my lady did a good deal of talking about her son, who had grown into a strong, good-looking nineteen-year-old man. Last summer she had spent an hour crying about the fact that he had just joined the marines. He had broached the subject the previous winter, asking her for permission to sign up early while he was still in high school, and still seventeen years old. She flatly refused as they argued on the phone, saying that once he was eighteen he could make his own decisions, but until then there was "no way she was signing her son over to them." For months, she repeatedly gave her reasons for him not entering the military.

"You weren't raised to be a sheep, or a soldier. Are you ready to kill little kids? Keep us safe from what? You don't like being told what to do, but once you sign on that line they own you. I don't think you get the full implications." My lady even threatened to go on a hunger strike. However when, on his eighteenth birthday, he informed her that he had signed the enlistment papers she abruptly dropped the argument.

"I still absolutely object; I fought him every step of the way. But he's doing what he thinks is right; just because I don't agree doesn't make *me* right. Now that he has committed there's nothing I can do but support him. I don't want him hesitating or being distracted from doing all he needs to do to survive because of something we argued about. As smart and aware as he is, he really has no idea what he's in for or what this will do to him. This is gonna suck a lot at times and he needs to know that, no matter what, he can call me and not have to worry about me nagging him or making judgements. I'll give him shit when he gets home!"

She tried to joke; then she burst into tears. After a moment they breathed together.

Her son had come out to visit us for a week before he left for boot camp. He had been working out and had become very muscular. His hair was now about a quarter of an inch of reddish-blonde fuzz and he already looked very much like the marine he was soon to become.

I sensed a variety of emotions during that week. He spoke of being excited about the prospects that lie ahead of him, she spoke of being thrilled that he was here with us. They both laughed and smiled a lot. And they were both scared; there was no way they could mask that scent.

During her son's visit my lady's parents traveled from Ohio to visit with their daughter and grandson. They had just called and said they were heading down G Street.

"They're here! Come on let's go down stairs," my lady exclaimed when she hung up the phone, and we went down to the front sidewalk to wait for them.

It was obvious, to this canine, that they were her parents. The father had a sense of humor and wicked laugh that were much like my lady's, and the mother paid more attention to me than she did to the other humans in the room. Her father was a man that I would call a gentleman; he had a respectful, considerate way about him when he was around his wife and daughter. Her mother smiled and laughed a lot, and she talked with her hands, using gestures and facial expressions similar to my lady's.

For a few days my lady and her son walked around town and by the river with her folks. They laughed and chatted as they window-shopped and her dad took movies. I could sense my lady's embarrassment about all the second-hand clothing and furniture, and because she could not afford to properly entertain her family while they visited. However, she perked up like a small child when her mother brought out the party decorations and little extras she had brought to celebrate my human's birthday.

One afternoon, after her folks had gone, my lady returned from the library with an armful of DVD's of some her favorite television series. Except for daily walks along the river, we did not leave the apartment for the rest of the week, as they held a "science fiction marathon."

After a year in training, her son was being deployed to a place called Afghanistan. I remember the day he called and told her where he was going; I could hear him on the speaker phone. She put her hand over her mouth and tears began streaming down her reddening face. I put my head, heavily, in her lap and her breathing started again.

He flew out to Colorado to visit with his mom during a three-day "pre-deployment leave." I sensed a new strength and confidence in her son that overshadowed his fear. My lady smiled and kept herself calm by practicing the breathing exercises that were taught to her by the lady therapist, but the scent of her terror was unmistakable.

Shortly after her son's deployment, I heard my lady talking with Choowii's human. She told her that she had received some money from something called Social Security. Because of her mounting physical pains and challenges, and because she still had difficulty leaving our home without having an anxiety attack, she would now be receiving a small monthly income. She was excited. My lady wanted to visit her mom, dad and brother out in Ohio, and now we could. For the past couple of years, she had also been envisioning a homestead for us; she had been drawing and writing about the life she wanted. Now it was time to travel to a few places she had picked out, to see where it felt right to settle down.

My green-eyed human bought a tent and found a little blue pick-up truck, and loaded the bed with what we would need to survive on the road. The truck became her sanctuary. Just as with the apartment, my lady made the truck--which would soon have a camper--into a perfect, comfy little home. I enjoyed this time very much. Our new home was definitely cramped; however, my lady would park in places where we were able to enjoy rivers, or lakes or redwood forests, and not be surrounded by people. So we spent a great deal more time outside. Before we got a camper on the back of the truck, we slept in a large tent; she had a cot for herself and had gotten a nice cozy bed for me. I always loved our time spent in nature; it was much more comfortable away from all the man-made noises, smells and electronic signals. And I could see the healing effect it had on my lady.

Before we began our new adventure we stopped by to speak with the lady therapist. When we walked into the office I took my usual place under the desk, then changed my mind. The emotions in the office no longer caused me discomfort. Actually, it had begun to feel quite enjoyable. Rather than feelings of pain, remorse and frustration, the room now filled with determination, laughter and joy as she envisioned the life ahead of us. Her eyes shone as she shared what she saw.

"I can picture a lot of it. It's weird; there are some things that pop into my head involuntarily each time I think about my home; this just reinforces my knowledge that the stuff is already part of my life, but some things are still in my future.

"One thing is a wall of wood. It's just a tall wood-panelled wall in the living room. Also, I can feel and hear the gravel crunching beneath my feet as I walk to the greenhouse. And I can see it. I can see the path and the greenhouse ahead--and further down the path is a shed."

"That's wonderful," smiled the therapist. "I really think it's great that you're doing this. What about the other things that you are manifesting?"

"Oh, it's going to be awesome!" My lady giggled and excitedly rattled off all that came to her head, like a person who just drank too much coffee.

"Except for seeing that there will be a lot of wood, stone and deep-blue tiles, I don't really know what the house will look like, but I know what it will have. There is an attached greenhouse and sunroom, besides the separate one that I mentioned. In it there is a hot tub and a shower, and a sitting area with a firepit. All surrounded by various edible plants. I can see enough firewood piled up to keep us warm for a few winters. I have fruit trees and berry bushes. There are rain barrels to collect water for the crops. I have solar and turbine power, and I have a clean reliable water source. There are out-buildings--like maybe it's an old farm or something--so that travelers can stay when they need shelter. It's sitting on forty acres and the acre surrounding the house and gardens is fenced in. There is a room or building reserved for my son, and he will never be homeless again. The house is heated with wood and ambient heat, and it has a large comfy kitchen for cooking, canning and hanging out with friends. There is a door in the kitchen, that leads to the attached greenhouse where I go out and pick things for meals. I see a fire pit and a large area for drum circles, and I can see that it is decorated with lapis-blue tiles and lots of edible plants and flowers. Oh, and there's an outhouse; and all toilets are composting."

****

Chapter Fourteen

$\mathcal{D}$uring our travels we had been invited to stay with her friend from Denmark, who now lived in Comptche, California, when she found out that we would be on the coast for a while to wait for our boy to return from Afghanistan. We were going to stay in the tent in her yard. However, given the wet weather, she suggested we stay in the converted chicken coop instead, where we'd be up off the ground and have better protection from the rain. It had been converted into a small pottery shop which was temporarily unused and perfect for our needs.

About fifty feet from the chicken coop was her friend's house. She told us it had originally been the goat house. Her friend had rebuilt it and made a very cozy home. The tub and shower were outside on a deck, and a short path led to an outhouse amongst the trees.

The woman's young black cat, Lucy, and I hit it off immediately. I loved her. She was not at all afraid of me. We ran through the yard and surrounding meadows and wrestled in the tall grass throughout the entire visit, while my lady and her friend sat and talked for hours, laughing like I've heard young girls laugh.

It was the most relaxed I had seen her in a very long time. She had become so much happier since she hasn't been weighed down by feelings of fear, and remorse about the past. There was a new strength to her--a quieter, more durable strength. Even the man that smelled bad couldn't take it from her.

We passed him as my lady pulled into the shopping plaza in Ft. Bragg to pick up a few groceries. He was on foot and on his way out of the parking lot. She just rolled her eyes.

"Good, he's leaving." She smiled at me and scratched my ear. My human pulled her, rarely-used, tag out of the glove compartment and hung it on the mirror, then parked in the handicapped spot so I'd be in full view and close to the door of the market--"just in case." While she was inside her ex-husband doubled back and came in the other entrance to the plaza and I saw him head into the grocery store. There was nothing I could do to warn her. She emerged a few minutes later with the groceries. I could see her hands tremble as she tried to get the key into the ignition.

"Geez, Ebby. He's so predictable; he walked right toward me as I was going to check out. We made eye contact, and I rolled mine as he passed me within inches." She paused and wrung her hands. "Wow, I'm really shaking. Shit. What's that about? I'm not upset, I feel no anxiety, nothing." I sensed no fear, just some frustration.

A few days later we met her friend that smelled like cloves, his son, and his brother for breakfast. She pulled into the parking lot of the train depot in town after seeing no parking spaces in front of the restaurant. However, after seeing the man that smells bad in walking through that lot, she sighed and asked the sky, "Seriously? How does he *do* that," and went back and waited for a spot by the entrance. When she came out an hour later she was laughing and hugging her friend. She smelled like waffles and maple syrup when she got in the truck so I sat up and looked at her expectantly.

"Oh, sorry Ebby." She made a guilty face. "I didn't save you any; I couldn't help it, it was really good!"

My lady then drove directly down into the Noyo Harbor "to make up for it." At the seaside entrance to the harbor was one of the few areas on the coast where I could run around without a leash. The beach was covered with rocks, driftwood and long tubes of seaweed with bulbs at the ends. I don't like the waves and salt water as much as I enjoy the river with it's constant flow and no surprises. However, I do enjoy the sounds of the waves pounding the sand, the melancholy fog horn and the seagulls calling to each other.

I grabbed rocks from the waves as my lady talked on the phone with her mother. They had been talking for about twenty minutes when my lady exclaimed.

"Oh my goodness, I forgot! I saw him--twice. Yeah, and I totally forgot about it! How cool is that? When I first saw him I was shaking, but my therapist told me that I may have body memories, sometimes. The next time I didn't shake at all. And I totally forgot about it until just now! No more fear, no more power over me! Mom, this is amazing!"

Winter was nearing and it was getting colder, and we had to find warmer accommodations than the chicken coop. We were on the north coast and, even though we were out of the snowy Rocky Mountains, if we stayed somewhere as far inland as Comptche we probably would see snow. Also, the lady who owned the property wanted to use the coop, which was actually her pottery shed, so there was a time limit.

Our hostess spoke with her friends to see if anyone had a place to rent and my lady answered ads and asked the sky for assistance. With the truck packed, on the day we were to leave for parts unknown, my lady placed her lapiz wand on the dash board and said, "Thank you for guiding us to shelter." As she was climbing up into the driver's seat her friend came out the door of her home.

"Guess what! That was my friend from Laytonville on the phone. He has a trailer for rent and needs help with his gardens.

Good timing, huh?" She glanced at the lapiz wand on the dashboard and grinned as she handed my lady a piece of paper with directions to the next place we would stay.

"I love when that happens." My lady laughed and looked at the paper. "Spy Rock Road," she read out loud and looked at her friend. "Is it close to town or is it isolated? I mean, is it safe for the two of us to be there? Will I have a phone signal?"

"Oh, it's a bit isolated, but he's not too far from the main road. I don't know about a signal, but it's safe, I assure you." The woman's grin made my lady squint her eyes with suspicion.

"Okay, what's the catch? Is this guy really creepy or something?"

"I don't have creepy friends," she objected, "Honestly, no catch. You'll see when you get there; you're going to love it. It's quite beautiful."

Following the directions, my lady drove through a small town and turned onto the street with the missing street sign, ascending along a curvy, tree-lined road.

"This is it. Wow," she said as we pulled through the open gate and she parked next to a long camper. As we stood outside the truck her eyes were bright; she broke into a huge smile as she looked around. It really was gorgeous, and there were so many exquisite new smells.

My lady and I stood on top of a mesa and looked down upon tiers of gardens. There were flowers, corn, berry bushes and trees. At the lowest point, dissecting the property, was a creek and past that was the main house, surrounded by more flower and vegetable gardens. So many trees, so many acres to run on, and so many wild turkeys to chase! It was late autumn but most of the trees were evergreens so it looked like lush green velvet lining the ravine at one end of the land.

The greenhouse was on this side of the creek, on the mesa with the camper; it held three large black tubs, six feet in diameter. In them were the remnants of what must have been at least ten-foot-tall cannabis plants. The smell was still strong. It's a pungent aroma that reeks of skunk just enough to wrinkle my nose; but I can't resist sniffing it again and again, as it has a certain sweetness to its scent. Having been harvested within the last two weeks, it was now my lady's job to go in an clean up all the debris that had been left--pulling stumps and clearing the way for next spring's planting. Outside, and a few tiers down and toward the creek, there were at least a dozen holes the same size as the tubs in the greenhouse. The musical-voiced lady's friend, the man who owned the property, told my lady that she could work off the rent of the trailer and from what I could see there was enough work to last until it was time to drive to Camp Pendelton, when our boy returned from Afghanistan.

During our stay here there were frequent calls from her son. Among other things they discussed, he explained that he was a part of the Second Battalion, Fourth Marine Regiment and they were in a place called Helmand Province, Afghanistan, from September, 2011 to March, 2012. The Fourth Marine Regiment was nicknamed the "Magnificent Bastards." Years ago, the regiment had been under the command of an army general who chose to surrender during battle. It was scattered in disgrace as punishment and only exists as attachments to other regiments; hence, they are "bastards." They are some of the most heroic and daring of the marines; hence, they are "magnificent."

Because of the time difference he usually called at about two a.m. There was only one spot in the camper where there was a phone signal. The phone, therefore, had to sit on a counter in the kitchen area. This was several feet from the foot of my lady's bed. Try as she may she was not able to keep it warm in this camper so she slept in a sleeping bag on one twin bed and I slept on the other bed across the aisle, snuggled in my coat. One night the phone rang and I watched as she struggled to get out of the bag, but the zipper was jammed. She was partially out of the bag and hurried to the phone. She got tangled, lost her balance and down she went, about two feet short of the counter. The phone stopped ringing and she started cursing with frustration as she pulled at the bag. Then it began to ring again.

He had called back, saying "just thought I should try again." Right then and there, they agreed that he'd always call twice, because she's kind of clutzy.

My lady would put the phone on speaker, heat up some cocoa and smoke some of the Emerald Triangle's finest cannabis to ease the pain in her joints as he'd tell her of the day's events. There was a lot of laughter; she said he was able to take the scariest event and put a funny slant on it. There were other times when she'd listen with her hand over her mouth and her eyes wide with fear and welling with tears. When the conversation was over; she would get down on her knees and thank the ceiling for "watching over him and holding him in it's light."

"Almost got in trouble yesterday," he said sheepishly through the phone speaker one night.

"Oh great," she chuckled. "What did you do?"

"Well, I was walking from the showers to the gym, and in between are the dog kennels. I saw Sargent O.J. sitting there; he's a black lab. When he saw me looking at him he started wagging his tail and I thought, 'Fuck it; why not?' I looked around and didn't see anyone, so I went over and was rubbing his ears and saying, 'good boy' when the First Sargent came around the corner."

"Oh no! Ahaha," my lady laughed.

"Yeah, so he yells, 'Hey!' I jumped up and stood at parade rest. I was scared; petting the dogs is a definite no-no by anyone but that dog's handler. And they make them sargents so that their handlers will be facing a court marshal if they abuse them in any way.

"'Do you know that that dog is your superior," he yelled.

"'Yes, First Sargent!'

"'Then why are you petting him?' I opened my mouth but could think of nothing to say. Something was watching over me, because he just yelled, 'You dumb fuck; get away from those dogs,' and he walked away."

He and my lady were laughing together when he remembered something else.

"Oh, haha! The other day we were hanging out and we were bored so we started picking through some unopened boxes of supplies when we came across a whole box of kevlar underwear."

"Ahaha, what?"

"Basically, they're cammoflage diapers. The thing is, we're in the desert and these combat undies are for jungle fighting so they really stand out here and make our junk a target. Anyway, one of my buddies gets naked and puts a pair on, then starts running around the patrol base, hooting and hollaring, and fucking with the guys on post.

"The C.O. yells to us, 'Tackle that fucking marine now!' But, we saw how much fun he was having so we decided to join him instead."

One morning, as she was in the bathroom and I was lying on the floor in the living area, a mouse ran from one corner to another. I jumped up to check it out and it ran towards me! I wasn't sure what to do so I ran--and the thing chased me! When I got to the bed area I had run out of room. It was either run face-first into the closed bathroom door at the end of the small corridor or jump on my bed. The latter seemed like the smartest move.

With me out of the way, the mouse just kept running forward, right under the bathroom door and, I gather, head-first into my lady's feet. Her blood-curtling scream reminded me of the many horror movies we had watched together. It must have scared the mouse because he came zipping back out from under the door and disappeared under a cabinet. I heard the toilet flush and the door was flung open.

"Oh! A lot of help you are! Ya big coward," she exclaimed when she saw me on my bed.

The mice must have liked the camper, because they made their home under our beds, and scratched and ran around under us all night long. After a few months we were both pretty stressed by the huge rodent population. They were clearly the alpha creatures in this domain. It was nearing the time when her son would be returning from Afghanistan, so we headed back down to Comptche and stayed with her friend again for a few days as we waited for her son's call. By this time the weather was warming up a little so the coop was comfortable again.

"So where are you heading after you pick him up?" We were all outside; Lucy and I were wrestling and our humans sat on the deck drinking tea and smoking a joint.

"I've been talking to a friend from Salida. She has bought some land in Saguache; it's near Crestone, where they supposedly have all kinds of UFO sightings. It's high altitude desert, but the land is cheap and if you have something to live in, you can take time and build a pretty sweet homestead. My other friends are building a home right now; they make their own cob bricks and everything," she paused when her friend made a face.

"Have you seen some of these houses? They're beautiful! When they're done, they just look like adobe. They're extremely energy efficient and you can choose whatever shape you want. Honestly, some are gorgeous. Anyway, it's two hundred dollars a month for the land, and no down payment. At that price, I can afford to live on the land for a little while and see if we like it. I can picture some of my homestead, I just don't know where it's going to be yet." She paused and thought.

"I do know I don't want to be in California or Ohio," my lady continued, "which means I've narrowed the location down to Colorado."

"How did you get into this law of attraction stuff? Did someone tell you about it, or did you see it on the internet or something," her friend from Denmark asked.

"When I was a kid my grandfather died. He had been bedridden for a long time after a series of strokes. It was pretty gruesome and my brother and I had a hard time with the situation. We both suffered from anxiety. I started having attacks at night, right after the funeral. Also, his was the first dead body I'd ever seen and the whole mortality thing hit me hard. The thought that I could one day just cease to exist terrified me. I used to call out to my mom for help.

One night, my mom sent my dad in to talk to me because she just didn't know what to do to help me anymore. He sat with me and spoke for hours of different realms our Spirits travel to after leaving this plane. He was talking me down from the attack, but he also planted a seed as he talked about how we are so much more than we can see with our limited human sight.

"When I was in my mid-teens he gave me a heavy, overwhelming-looking book called *Science of Mind*, which teaches about the law of attraction. I didn't get it. I'd try to read it, then I'd put it away and bring it back out every so often. Years later I looked to it for answers when I was no longer able to be powerless in that twelve-step program.

"A couple of years ago I saw *The Secret* on DVD at the library and realized it was essentially the same thing. I had come to understand the book, but it wasn't until I saw that movie that something clicked, and I began to really practice the principles. You can borrow it if you like; it really is very empowering."

"So you just imagine what you want and it comes to you," her friend asked. I definitely detected a tone of disbelief.

"Well, that's oversimplified, but basically--yes. You envision what you want, then thank the Universe for bringing it to you. The key is to truly know that what you have requested will manifest, and to feel the gratitude and joy when putting it out there because you already know it's part of your life.

"There are things I see each time I imagine what my homestead will be like. For the past couple of years, when I think about my home I immediately see a tall wall of wood. It's weird, it's not something I choose to see, the image always just pops into my head. I can see myself listening to music in a room with this wall. Other times, I can hear and feel the gravel crunching beneath my sandals as I walk on a path near the greenhouse. I see that the greenhouse has a shower and a sitting area with a fire pit. When an image comes easily or involuntarily like that, I know that it is already a part of my future and I feel the gratitude. And the more gratitude I feel, the more I have to be grateful for. It's pretty cool!"

Every night now, for about a week, my lady had been thanking the corregated roof of the chicken coop for bringing us a camper shell for the truck before we left to get her son. Then today she spoke to someone on the phone for a bit, saying that she'd be there tomorrow. She told her friend with the musical voice that we'd be gone for the day.

Her friend objected, saying that that was a long way to go to get ripped off, and that there was no guarantee that it'll be the one in the picture. She was also concerned about our safety.

"In the picture it looks perfect for what I need. Worst case we just go for a nice drive and come home the same as we left. And I have Ebony with me so I'm safe. Right Ebby?" My lady questioned me and I wagged my tail.

"Okay, if you say so." Her friend shook her head.

"I can feel it. For the past few days, as I drove I could actually feel the camper on the back already. I know I'm getting it."

"Okay." She put up her hands in surrender.

When we rode up the driveway that evening, camper shell secured to the bed of the pick-up, her friend walked out with her hands on her hips, grinning.

"Sweet, huh," my lady smiled when she got out of the truck. Her friend inspected the camper as she circled the truck and returned to where we stood.

"I think I do want to borrow that DVD," her friend said as we walked into the house.

Once her son had called and said he was heading home from a place called Camp Leatherneck, my lady and I headed down the coast. The phone call was a surprise; he was originally scheduled to return almost a month from now. However, he said he was assigned to something called an "advon party." He was to accompany some other men and arrive back home three weeks early to ready the barracks and supplies for the rest of the men's return. This was wonderful, but it did mean that the reception at Camp Pendelton would be less spectacular than if the entire battalion was returning.

My lady had parked in the closest spot possible and I was able to watch her through the window of the truck, although it was now completely dark out. There were a few floodlights on the parade deck, but it was mostly shadowed.

Under the lights, I could see the crowd turn in unison at the sound of any engine; then they all turned back and chuckled when the people saw that it was not their sons arriving. The air sizzled with excitement as the families waited.

From the darkness came the suddenly deafening roar of about two dozen motorcycles as the marines' escort emerged from the black and slowly rode into the area where everyone stood. People began to cheer and wave. The bikers circled around and parked out of the way.

The engines were quieted and there was a seemingly unending pause as the crowd got very still; everyone appeared to be holding their breath as they looked expectantly into the darkness from whence the motorcycles emerged. Then there was another sound, a syncronized beat from the darkness--smack, smack, smack, smack. And it was getting louder. Just when I realized that it was many boots hitting the pavement in unison, row by row the faces of the young men appeared under the street lights. They were pressed, dressed and preened; they looked so straight and tall.

I couldn't see her son, but I felt he was there. The cheering had become almost as loud as the motorcycle engines. They marched until they were all standing on the parade deck, then they were ordered to turn and face the tear-stained grins of their families. In a moment they were released with a shout from a commanding officer and there was instant chaos--crying, laughing, hugging and flashes of light from pictures being taken.

I started to feel concern. Through it all, I could feel her rising discomfort at being in the center of a crowd. I could see her whirling around, searching the camouflaged uniforms and shaved heads for her son. Then, just before the panic took hold, she stopped. She got very still in the midst of the chaos, closed her eyes, took a deep breath, and began to *bellow* his last name--enabling our young man to hone in on his mom's voice and find her within seconds.

When her son's leave came to an end, he went back to Camp Pendelton and we returned to Colorado. We did wind up in Saguache, which is about an hour south of Salida. I could hear her mother on the phone, putting my exact sentiments into words.

"You're moving to the desert? How are the two of you going to survive in those harsh conditions? This seems very dangerous to me."

"Mom, I want to check this out. I have a few friends doing the same thing. It's only $200 a month so I can afford to stay on the land for a bit to see if we like it. There are all kinds of possibilities!"

"You want to make a house out of straw," her mother said flatly.

"Have you ever seen a strawbale house? They can be really awesome; they're cheap and easy to build and energy efficient. I just need to feel this out. I need to see if this is where I want my homestead. And like I said, I won't be alone. It'll be great."

It was not great. However, my headstrong human insisted we endure life on the high plains desert of the San Luis Valley for three months. *Three months.* Three windy, dusty, hot, bug-ridden, vermin-infested, boring months. It wasn't until I refused to leave the truck to do anything but urinate and deficate that she allowed herself to admit that she, too, was completely miserable in the desert.

My lady tolerates and works with a situation, and gives it positive energy until her gut says "enough." One day, it was like a switch was flipped and she knew it was time to move on to the next experience, all the while envisioning the long-term outcome.

I was thrilled when we left the desert. We both need trees and water! Everything smells so bland in the desert. Water brings things to life and excites my senses. Back in Salida we spent days basking by the river's edge, soaking up all the moisture and greenery we had missed.

My lady and I spent a lazy summer and fall by the river and lakes in the area. At the end of the summer we drove out to Ohio to spend a little time with her parents and brother. Her son was also able to fly out during his leave. I swam in Lake Erie and my lady and her son swam in the pool at the motel. At night they'd eat junk food and watch DVDs until it was almost morning. They'd sleep for a few hours, then we'd head over to our family's house and spend several hours with them. Once her son returned to Camp Pendelton, my lady and I slept in the camper in her folks' driveway.

We stayed another week in Ohio and they all spent a lot of time talking and laughing. One after noon she and her mom and I were sitting under the tree, on the patio. They were discussing where we might go for the winter.

"I've been feeling like maybe I want to go north and check it out up there. Maybe go to Nederland; I liked it there. I'll just have to see when I get back; the right place will turn up." My lady told her mom.

"You're like a butterfly." Her mom smiled and shook her head.

"Um, thanks?"

"No, really. You travel around, you experience things, you taste the flowers along the way. You flutter here; then you flutter over there. It looks like you have no destination whatsoever. But you always get where you need to be."

My lady found a studio to rent in a motel in a town called Leadville after searching for a couple of months. It was run-down and there were several harmless drunks that would get loud some nights, but the people were all nice and we felt relatively safe. Living at over 10,000 feet was new for both of us. The lack of air and the huge amount of snow took a little getting used to. But we did, and we spent a fun winter, playing in the snow then warming up in our nice, cozy little room.

It was almost spring when the lady with the musical voice called and asked my human to return to California to watch her homestead as she visited her mother in Denmark. My human eagerly accepted, looking forward to being on land that she said felt healing and regenerative. We visited the lady therapist before we left for the coast. In a previous session they were both surprised to find that my lady felt no charge of emotion when she finally relented and held the buzzies to clear out the feelings about the man that smelled bad. The therapist told my lady that she had had a "universal healing." She had done all the necessary work, and having processed everything else, the feelings about her ex-husband were sort of flushed away with the rest of it. It turned out that there was no reason to relive any of it.

"And now," she encouraged my lady, "it's time for you to go out an enjoy your life. You have a good idea about what you want--so go get it."

It felt good to be back here in what my lady's friend called the "hassle free zone." This was a remarkably peaceful place, where my lady was able to spend more time in nature, with no distractions. Instead of street sweepers and garbage trucks, the noises here came from frogs, turkeys, bugs and a menagerie of other wild creatures. I love it here; this is one of my favorite places to be, right up there with the Arkansas River. There were three of us here right now--my lady, Lucy, and myself.

"This is great," my lady had said to me when she hung up the phone. "We'll be on the coast for when my son's released from the Marines. Maybe we can even go and get him!"

My lady's son was being "medically retired." She had talked to her mom on the phone and tried to explain what was happening.

"I don't have all the facts. Basically, he is being retired from the Marines for two reasons. He is having nightmares and flashbacks, and he is having difficulty dealing with stress since he's been back. Among other things, he has been diagnosed with PTSD.

"And they really pushed his poor body to the limit. When he was in-country he said his gear weighed up to 300 pounds. So his hips, knees and ankles are all screwed up from carrying all the weight, and he is actually a couple of inches shorter now. Several explosions have caused traumatic brain injuries, so he's having problems stemming from that, also."

We were in for a wonderful surprise when we picked up her son. He said that he would like to come to Colorado and live with us for a while. My lady was beside herself with excitement as they made plans during the drive up the coast, to Ft. Bragg.

****

CHAPTER FIFTEEN

*W*e all stayed at Raven's Fall so her son could spend time with his dad, uncle, and buddies before we left for Colorado. My lady and I were in the camper, parked amongst the tall redwoods; her son slept in his room in the house. She would sit on the tailgate of the truck, swinging her legs and grinning at how peaceful and green it was. For the most part the only sounds were from the birds; several different songs woke us each morning. And there were plenty of ravens, but they didn't sing. Sometimes they would caw, they just usually seemed to be laughing at us.

I wasn't allowed to run around as much as I would have liked because there were two, very large dogs living there. Their names were Ojo and Heiny and they thought that *my* boy was *their* boy. They were both pups when they came to live here so I could understand the mistake, but really, short of peeing on him I couldn't have marked my territory more clearly. Anyway, we didn't get along, so when they were out running around, I had to be inside the truck.

The two dogs came out to greet everyone the afternoon we arrived. I was in the camper and they hadn't seen me yet. Ojo, a large rottwheiler, passed too closely to the truck so I snarled and barked and slammed into the side of the camper as I struggled to see out window, making the truck rock slightly. This sent that huge dog running all the way back to the house in fear; had she still had a tail, it would have been between her legs. Ahaha! And the look on her mug a few days later, when she saw how small I really am, was priceless.

Late Sunday morning, June 9, 2013, were sitting in the truck, out at Todd's Point. My green-eyed lady was alternately watching the seagulls and writing in her journal when the phone rang. She put the device on speaker and propped it up on the steering wheel.

"Hey sis, it's me," his voice was strained; even through the phone I could tell something was wrong.

"What happened?" She heard it, too.

"It's dad. He's okay, but he's in the hospital because he was having trouble with his heart."

"Oh my god, is it bad? Is he going to be okay? How is mom? Is she okay?"

"He's okay. Mom's fine. The worst is over ..."

"What do you mean, 'the worst is over?' Tell me what happened," she insisted.

He did not go into great detail but he updated her, the best he could, on the events of the past several hours. Then she asked if he was okay.

"Yeah, I'm just drained. It was pretty awful, sis ..." his voice broke and it took a moment for him to recover. "He was dead. Mom did CPR; she saved him. But he was *dead*." The last word came out as a whisper.

The following day, she spoke with her mom, who filled in the exact details about what had happened. My lady sat silently and listened as the tears rolled down her face. She lit a cigarette, then made a nasty face and put it out immediately.

I could hear her mom's weary voice on the speaker as she told us what happened. And it was easy to picture the events unfolding as she described them. She said it was early Sunday morning and they were getting ready to go to church …

"Hon, we're going to be late; what's taking you so long this morning?" she asked as she applied her lipstick, looking in a small spot she had wiped dry in the steamy bathroom mirror.

"I don't feel very well," he said weakly, as he sat down on the couch. Her mother put down the lipstick and hurried out into the living room when she heard the sound of his voice, and when she saw his face she went to the top of the stairs and called down to her son, who was still sleeping in his basement bedroom.

"I need you! Something's wrong with your father; please come up here," she yelled to her son who ascended the stairs two at a time while his mom called 911; as she began to speak to them she heard a noise, a noise that she said would give her chills the rest of her days. She said it sounded like a loud mournful snore; then her son cried out as if he was in physical agony.

"DAD! DAD, WAKE UP! DAD!"

She ran into the living room and saw that her husband had stopped breathing, then ran back to the phone she had left dangling.

"He's not breathing," she panted. The young man on the other end of the phone instructed her to begin CPR until the rescue team arrived.

Again she dropped the phone and ran back to the living room where her son was holding his father's head in his lap. She pushed him aside.

"They said I have to do CPR," she exclaimed as she began to compress her husband's chest. Until the team arrived, this seventy-six-year-old woman, who stood just under five foot three inches, and who had had open heart surgery a few years prior, had the strength to keep her husband's heart pumping for several minutes.

"Come on, Hon ... don't you dare leave me," she commanded. "You breathe!"

In the ambulance, he was attached to a Lucas Machine which took over pumping his chest. From the house to the hospital, my lady's mom said they "zapped" him seven times. Once they were at the hospital, he was transferred to the machine there.

One hundred times per minute, compressing his chest a full two inches each time, the machine cracked and bruised every one of his ribs as it mercilessly, tirelessly pumped his chest and kept his blood flowing for an hour and ten minutes, at which point the doctor came out into the waiting room and told his family that since they had had no response for over an hour, they were going to turn off the machine. He apologetically suggested the family go in and say goodbye.

The doctor left the family alone to collect themselves--and he burst back through the door moments later.

"He's responding!" The doctor laughed and put his hands in the air, palms up, indicating that he was dumfounded.

My lady said she knew her dad was going to be okay. Last week he had been talking to her about a few things he wanted to do and "he was too stubborn to go anywhere until he did them."

He was the one who had introduced her to the law of attraction and manifesting things in our lives. During one visit I remember hearing him tell the story about how he had seen a man playing a magnificent organ in a place called Atlantic City, during a "masonic convention." Her father did not know how to play any keyboard, yet he said he was able to see himself doing it. He said he just knew that he was going to play that organ. He got himself an electronic keyboard and, without any lessons, taught himself to play, repeatedly trading keyboards in for larger, more advanced, models.

My human had chimed in here and laughed, remembering the three-tier church organ that sat in the living room of their small second floor apartment in Kenilworth, New Jersey. He practiced all the time. Like his daughter he had carpal tunnel, but cracked, bleeding, painful fingers did not stop him. I imagine that Cindy, the dog that was a part of their family at the time, could feel same determination that I can sense in my lady when she makes up her mind.

The day came, in 1977, when he sat at that great organ, having been made Organist for the Grand Lodge of New Jersey, just like he knew he would.

My human's mom later explained that her husband had suffered a cardiac arrest, which meant that his heart had had an electrical short. She said the doctors referred to it as hitting the "reset button."

"It really is a miracle that he is still alive." She told her daughter. "There were a number of things that had to fall into place for him to survive. It could have happened on Monday and I would have been at work, for one thing. But also, we wanted him to go to another hospital but this one's emergency team got the call--and it turns out the other hospital doesn't have a Lucas Machine, and they said they would have stopped doing CPR after twenty minutes on a person your father's age. Your dad has asked the staff a few times, why they kept going for so long."

"What did they say?"

"They all just kind of shrugged and said they weren't sure, but they just knew they didn't want to stop."

"Wow." My lady was visibly moved. "He must have more to do."

"Oh my goodness, that's exactly what your father said when he woke up!"

"How does he seem? Is it okay to talk to him?"

"Well, you can try, but they have him on a lot of drugs right now and he's kind of ... well, actually he's pretty crazy." Her mom stated. "When he woke up he complained to the nurse that I had 'beaten the crap out of him' when I did the CPR."

"Doesn't he know about the machine?" My lady laughed.

"He keeps forgetting things, like you did after you came out of the coma; it'll take a while. In the mean time, we're having fun! I'll hit speaker-phone and put it on his table so you can talk."

Her father had been in the hospital a few times before for various procedures; she said she always thought he was pretty funny when he was on drugs, saying that since he rarely takes even aspirin, he has a very low tolerance and even the smallest dosage can send him to a place called Wonderland.

"Hey Dad, how's it going?"

"Oh, okay." We could hear that he was smiling, albeit weakly.

"I hear you're getting some pretty good drugs!"

"Ahaha, *cough-cough*. Yeah, I don't know which end is up. I don't like not being in control; it feels very unsettling. And I don't like this place at all."

"Why not?"

"Well, you'd think they'd keep it cleaner. There are a lot of bugs; I can see them running up the wall from here."

My lady's hand flew up to cover her mouth and stifle the laughter before she responded.

"I know, not being in control is a scary feeling. But try to look at it this way: You are in a perfectly safe place, lots of people are watching over you, and you're not leaving your bed so nothing bad is going to happen. Just let your head entertain you. Really Dad, people pay good money to feel the way you do right now."

In the background we could hear her mother. "Oh, good heavens!"

Her father chuckled and began coughing uncontrollably.

"Okay, you can't talk to him anymore. All his ribs are cracked, and you're making him laugh. You can't see it but he's wincing over here," her mother chastized.

"Bye dad," my lady yelled and laughed at the phone right before we heard it disconnect.

Later she and her son were sitting on the tailgate of the truck talking, while I lay on my lady's bed. She told her son what happened to her father, and how her mom had performed CPR.

"Honestly, I don't know how she does some of the things she does," my lady marveled.

"Yeah, she's a pretty bad-ass grandma," her son laughed.

During our stay in Ft. Bragg, if she wasn't making lists or thanking the sky, my lady was on the phone with people in a place called Longmont, CO. She and her son had picked that area because of the colleges in that town and in nearby Boulder, and because her son said he didn't want to live in the "boonies." She spoke with realtors regarding a house for them to rent. Every time she made any efforts to find a home in that area, I could sense her anxiety and irritablilty, and she'd been complaining of pains in her abdomen. Besides that, she was having no luck. I watched her frustration as every avenue she tried seemed to come to a dead end.

"Okay, when I feel like this and I keep running into roadblocks it usually means that I need to try another direction." She said to her son one afternoon. "Since we are having no luck in that area, why don't we try somewhere else for a bit?"

Being more familiar with the area, she made some calls to people in Leadville and was able to find a temporary rental immediately in the motel where we had stayed the previous winter. Once we got back to Colorado, we got settled in and she began to search for places to live between Leadville and Salida.

Over the radio, one morning, came news of the flash floods in the Longmont area, devastating cities for miles around.

"See? I knew there was something wrong about going there," she slapped her belly and laughed. "We just gotta trust the gut." Then she looked at the ceiling and thanked it.

After speaking with realtors and answering advertisements, my lady spoke with a man whom she said owned over fifty rental properties in Leadville. We all piled in the truck and met this man she called a "landlord." Since arriving here, my lady's son said he'd like to have his best friend come and live with them--which would help with expenses--so they were looking for a three-bedroom house. The first two houses we looked at did have three bedrooms, but my humans just wrinkled their noses when they left each one, indicating their disapproval. Then we drove to the last house on the list. It was up on a place the landlord called "Chicken Hill" and looked out over the rest of the town. There were three bedrooms, two of which were large while the third measured about eight foot by eight foot and could barely fit a bed, let alone furniture.

"Don't you love this? This is the place," my lady smiled as she looked around.

"Mom, it's nice, but there's no way I'm putting my friend in that tiny room." Her son replied as he pointed to the small room at the back of the house.

"This is where we're supposed to be," my lady insisted. Then she conceded. "Ebby and I will take the small room and you guys can have the large ones."

"Seriously, Mom, that's really small; you're not going to like it."

"Sweetie, I've been living in my truck for over a year. Yeah, the room is small. But I'll have a kitchen and a living room--in a real home! This will work."

"Okay, if you think so." Her son shook his head and smiled.

"I know so. I mean, the house has some definite drawbacks and it'll be a bitch to heat in the winter, but I feel this is where we're supposed to be." She paused and walked to front of the living room. Mts. Massive and Elbert filled the windows.

"Besides, look at this view! We're on the top of the world!" My lady's eyes sparkled as she took in the panorama.

We spent a quiet, relaxed couple of weeks getting used to our new home. We went to thrift stores and bought some furniture for the young men's bedrooms. My lady packed all of our personal things into our bedroom. She managed to fit her twin mattress, my bed, a dresser and a small desk into that tiny little space. Then she bought a door lock when her son's friend began inviting women he'd met on the internet into our home. There was not enough money to furnish the living room properly right away, so it just held a futon and a few deck chairs. I liked it because there was plenty of room to run around and play. Most of the time, my lady was in her room and the boys were in her son's room together playing video games.

I could feel that my human was becoming anxious; she seemed uncomfortable most of the time. I had been smelling a hormonal change in her body and could see the heat emanating from the back of her head, through her long thick hair, when she'd have a "hot flash." Her discomfort and frustration were obvious.

We'd drive up to a beautiful place called Turquoise Lake and I'd dive for rocks while she sat and talked to me. Only there could she breathe and relax.

"Geez, Ebby. I don't get it; this is what I wanted--a home in the mountains in Colorado. I know the menopause is making me irritable, but I just don't get why I'm not happy. I'm supposed to be happy now," she cried as she threw another rock for me to retrieve. In her anger the rock was propelled too far into the deep water. I stood still and looked at her.

"Sorry," she said when she saw my face, and lightly tossed another which landed much closer to shore. I ran to get it. With my head under water I could hear her muffled voice as she continued to cry.

"It's a nice house and my son is with me, but it just doesn't feel right. What am I missing?"

At the end of November a man that had been our neighbor at the motel the previous winter came to park his vehicle in our driveway for a while. He was an obsessive skier and needed a place to sleep at night while he skied daily, no matter the weather. He told us he had a plate in his head because he said he had "pulled a Sonny Bono" one year. I didn't know what that meant but the men all laughed as my lady shook her head at what she said was a distasteful joke. Although he was a bit odd, my lady said that he was always polite. He called her "Miss" all the time, and was a self-proclaimed "southern gentleman." She said he seemed safe. I didn't feel any clear danger; however, there was something phoney about him that made me uncomfortable. I just couldn't put my paw on it. She told him that he could make meals in the kitchen and use the shower, in exchange for him buying some food for them.

The arrangement did not go well. The man turned out to be more than a little unstable. He came in and tried to redecorate our home with things that looked as if they had been rescued from trash bins, like stained throw-rugs and faded event-posters. And although she gave him explicit lists, he bought meats and packaged foods that my lady could not, or would not, eat. And it appeared to this dog that he had been trying to install himself as the alpha male in the house. My human began to lock herself in our small bedroom whenever the "crazy-guy" entered the house. When he cleaned the brand new stick-free pans with steel wool one day she was livid.

"Why is he still in your home?" The lady therapist asked as my human complained to her on the phone. All it took was that one question. I watched my lady's face brighten at the idea that she could just tell him to leave. For some reason, as strong and independent as I knew she was, it seemed that she needed someone to give her permission to do certain things--as if she still did not entirely trust herself. Once the therapist asked the question my lady was instantly clear and resolved. She hung up the phone and knocked on her son's door.

"You don't have to say anything, but will you stand behind me, physically, as I tell him he has to leave?"

When the crazy-guy entered the house to make his breakfast we were waiting for him; she didn't need to ask me to stand at her side. My lady was polite as her son and I stood supporting her, and told the crazy-guy that the family felt that the arrangement was not working out.

"Okay. I just need a few days to find another place to park." He was smiling, but the veneer of this southern gentleman was thinning in spots and I could sense the pure rage that he was barely containing.

Then the man instantly went from "a little off" to "bat-shit-crazy" as he began to harrass the three of them--my lady, her son and his friend--on the telephone and internet, once he had left. Although they would all laugh incredulously at his unanswered messages, his behavior scared my lady. Her fear was palatable, although she knew that her son and I would protect her.

However, she was not afraid of his words and actions. She said she was afraid that she was still drawing the same type of people to her and could not understand why.

"Why is this still happening? Is the Universe testing me or something?" she exclaimed to the phone.

Through the speaker the therapist explained that she would not call it "testing;" it was more like she was being given opportunities to reinforce healthy practices. She was learning how to disengage and distance herself from the kind of energy he was exuding.

"So yes, there will still be people like him entering your life. But now you can recognize the signs--and you don't have to let those people stay. You can just brush them off and continue with your day," her therapist encouraged her. "One day you will wake up and realize that you don't even notice them anymore."

My lady's relief at the crazy-guy's absence was evident. However, her irritability had not decreased much. I watched as she'd force a smile when she'd leave our room to join her son and his friend for a meal or in the living room to chat. We had lived alone for so long, that being in such close quarters with anyone was bound to be a challenge for a while. Adding to both of our discomfort was the fact that her son had adopted a two-year-old Pitt Bull-Husky dog named Rocco.

It took me weeks to train the pup what was and wasn't acceptable in our home. He was completely non-aggressive, and he was clear on the fact that I was in charge. However, he was larger and much stronger than me and my lady was always afraid that he would hurt me, so she refused to ever leave us alone together. I was a little insulted, but I could feel her love as she tried to keep me safe. I could also sense she was resisting a growing affection for him. I understood the feelings and was not intimidated; he actually was kind of cute.

Then one day in late December it was all over. My lady's son sat her down at the kitchen table and said that he and his friend were returning to California.

"There's too much bickering," he complained. "Besides, I miss the coast; I miss Ojo and I miss my friends." He paused to take a deep breath. "And I really don't like the snow and the mountains--reminds me too much of Afghanistan. This just isn't working, Mom."

And, just like that, we were alone again.

Fortunately, we were not in danger of losing our home. Her son told her that he would continue paying half the rent, to fulfill the lease, and until she was able to find another roommate. As angry as she was, I could feel her beaming with respect for her son.

The next two weeks brought many tears and a few intense temper tantrums. Mostly she just walked from room to empty room and sobbed sloppily. I did my best to comfort her but she would have none of it. One evening she dropped to her knees in the middle of the living room and looked up and pled with the ceiling fan to answer her.

"Why? What am I not seeing? Spirit, please bring me clarity." She curled into a ball on her side and cried herself to sleep right there on the floor. There was nothing that I could do so I went into our room--which was now the master bedroom at the front of the house--and got comfy in my bed. A couple of hours later my lady came in, flopped onto her on bed and pulled the covers up over her head.

****

CHAPTER SIXTEEN

$\mathcal{T}$he following morning my green-eyed lady arose at four o'clock and let me out the front door to pee. Back inside she wiped the snow off my head, back and feet. Then she turned on the living room light on her way to the bathroom, stopped and slowly turned toward the wall behind the futon. It was one of those times when I got to watch that comic realization creep across her face. This time it was soon replaced with a smile--one that started with a tentative tug at the corners of her mouth and wound up brightening her sleepy eyes.

"It's the wall of wood," she said softly as her wide eyes stared ahead. "It's the *wall*."

She backed up and leaned against the front door. We had lived here for months, but my lady appeared to be seeing this wall for the first time. She sank to the floor and started crying, although it could have been laughter as the grin never left her face. I could feel intense joy and gratitude--as powerful as the rage that used to radiate from her. I had no idea what was going on, so I walked over to her and stuck my wet nose in her ear. She squealed and laughed louder.

"Ebby look! It's the wall!" With one arm she squeezed my neck as the other pointed to what stood in front of us. It was a nice wall I suppose, reaching to the high, vaulted ceiling. It was covered with pretty wooden paneling; and there were three, odd shaped, windows toward the top to let in the rising sun and moon lights. I didn't understand the commotion, but she was thrilled, so I was thrilled.

And, just like that, this house became our home. Everything felt different than it had the previous evening. My lady spent the next several days re-arranging furniture, sitting and standing in different spots around the house to be sure it felt good from every angle. Her son and his friend had left the things that had been purchased for their rooms, which now made the living room a comfy, welcoming place. The change was dramatic--in our home and in my lady. Suddenly, everything seemed to feel better and it felt as though everything was as it should be.

"It's time to write the book, Ebby," she announced as she put a tea bag in a cup and filled it with hot water from the whistling kettle.

I could feel that old determination and excitement as my lady walked in to her desk and turned on the computer. For the next six months, that's where she sat. Her desk was positioned so that she could write and look over the top of the screen at me laying on my bed under the window, and past me at Mt. Massive.

There were times when she'd burst out laughing at something she thought of. There were also many tears. I would think that, in order to properly convey what she experienced, she had to relive it all; she had to go back and dredge up all the feelings in order to be able to express them on paper. The harder she cried, the harder her fingers pounded at the keys. Tears ran down her cheeks and dripped onto the desk; she'd blink them away and refuse to stop until the scene in her head was transferred to the screen in front of her.

After a particularly emotional writing session she would stop and stretch. Then she'd make some more tea and, once the weather warmed up, take me outside for some fresh air. There she'd sit and breathe, and "shake off the negative stuff" as the mountain breezes blew past her. Sometimes a short break was all she needed, but several times it would take a day or two before she could return to the computer.

In the beginning she tossed and turned during the few hours when she found sleep each night. I can only assume she was wracked with processing and releasing what she had relived earlier that day, like she used to do in therapy. Toward the end of the first draft her sleep became more peaceful.

One afternoon in the spring we visited my lady's new doctor in Buena Vista. When she talked to her mother, I heard my lady explain that the medical clinic in Salida was closing so she now needed to go to the office in "BV." When my lady came out the door after her appointment she was grinning. She got in the truck and hugged me, then immediately called her mother.

"You're not going to believe this. This is very cool." My lady was almost laughing as she spoke. "I just saw the new doctor; she's great. She seems to get me and I felt pretty comfortable with her."

"That's great," her mother said through the speaker. "What did she say?"

"She told me that I have Temporomandibular Joint Disorder--TMJ, which is not great; however, it explains the headaches and pains in my jaw and neck. The cool part is that it also explains why I'm always hearing motors!"

"I don't understand."

"The doctor said that she also has TMJ, and during our visit she asked if I kept a fan on at night. She said that helps take the focus off of the humming in her ears."

"You're kidding! The TMJ makes you hear motors?"

"Yup. Ha! I'm not as crazy as I thought I was," my lady laughed.

After that visit, she also started taking a combination of herbs to relieve her "menopause moments." Once I could smell that her hormones were more balanced, I noticed her temperament had mellowed and she wasn't having as many hot flashes.

Conversations between my lady, her parents and her son, as they brainstormed for amusing memories to add to the book, brought a new healing. Once she felt confident that her family had forgiven her for her poor choices, and once she saw it all in black and white, she was finally able to finally look in the the mirror and forgive herself--and to feel a new, unshakable love for herself. I think my lady finally started seeing the woman that I saw that day when she came into the shelter and we rescued each other.

It's evening now, and I'm lying on my pillow at my lady's side while she stands in front of a group of women that I have never met before. I feel all sorts of emotions being emitted from the group. There's fear, anger, curiosity--and hope. Since her book was published, the telephone has been ringing quite a lot. Women have even called to ask my lady to come and talk with their "support groups."

"Me? I'm not a teacher or a therapist or anything. What is it you think I could possibly do," she asked in surprise the first time she was invited.

"You can come and tell us what you've experienced. Tell us about where you were, and where you are now--and tell us how you got there."

"That's it?"

"That's it. You will give hope and encouragement to women who are still in pain and don't know how to heal, or to women who think they are forever stuck in their present situations. Some of them truly believe that they deserve what they're getting from life."

"And that's why they keep getting it," my lady commented.

"You're right. Now, come and help me convince them of that fact."

My lady was silent. I could see that her mind was racing; her eyes darted around the room as she considered her response. She had spoken with her mother about wanting to help other women somehow; so I know this is what she wanted. Yet she was still very ill-at-ease around groups of people. She put her hand over the speaker.

"I'm gonna need your help," she said as she looked up at the ceiling.

"Excuse me," asked the woman on the other end of the phone line.

"Okay." My lady took her hand from the speaker. "Okay, I can do that."

Then she asked if she could call the woman back the next day, as she was on her way out the door. The fact of the matter, as she told her mother the next morning, was that she couldn't breathe, let alone discuss anything further with the woman. She needed to process what had just been put in front of her; she was excited and grateful--and terrified.

Then the night of her first speaking engagement arrived. My green-eyed lady, with the long, thick braid of graying red hair was standing behind a wooden podium; I could see her skirt vibrating as she trembled with anxiety. Over thirty women sat watching her, expectantly. She was supposed to be speaking, I think, but she was just standing there shaking, and I didn't see her breathing. I flicked my tail just enough to brush against the calf of her right leg. She jumped, inhaled quickly, and looked down at me. Then she smiled, took another breath--this time slow and deep--and returned her gaze to the small crowd.

"Hi." My human paused, looked out at the women, and chuckled. "Okay, this isn't working for me. You ladies mind if I sit down, so I can be a little closer to you? It's kind of scary up here."

With that she pulled my pillow up to the edge of the stage and plopped down beside me, her long skirt flowing over legs which dangled in front of her. She petted me as she began to speak. I could feel her discomfort begin to ease as she told of how her life used to be.

It warmed my heart to watch her. My lady's voice shook during the first moments; then she found her rythmn and her timber was strong and steady. She spoke of painful moments with unsmiling sincerity; those close enough to the stage could see the old heartache in her eyes, but her voice was unflinching as she recanted how she was brought to her knees by despair.

Then her tone changed and she began to beam as she talked about the healing, and the changes that had occurred in her life. She talked about the lady-therapist and of their work with EMDR therapy. Her eyes sparkled with gratitude when she spoke of the law of attraction, and how empowering it was to decide she wanted something, and to know that she had the power of the Universe at her disposal to make it happen.

"It wasn't easy, and it wasn't very pretty sometimes, I can assure you. I took a baseball bat into the woods on more than one occasion, and I yelled and pounded the earth until sheer exhaustion forced me to stop." She laughed and then got serious.

"And I did have to walk alone--for longer than I ever thought I could. There was no other way for me to find *Me*." She almost whispered the last word as she brought her hand to her chest.

"At the time I was too easily influenced by outsiders' energy, and hadn't the strength or where-with-all to set and fortify personal boundaries. I remained alone until it became what I wanted. And then I regaled in my solitude and protected it fiercely. It was just Ebby and me in our own little world as I healed and became who I am.

"Once I had progressed to a certain point, I began wanting some companionship and felt ready to start making some friends. So I expressed my desires to the Universe. Now I have a roommate--and he's not a whacko! He's a nice, normal, young man; his cats are a little evil, I think," she paused and winked at me. "But he seems to be relatively sane. There is also a young couple renting a parking space for their camper, on the property. Again, nice people--because those are the kind of people I now attract." She paused and took a sip of water.

"I used to think, 'People suck,' over and over in my head--and the people that came into my life did exactly that. Then I replaced the thought with, 'People that I like being around like being around me.'" She laughed and added, "I learned to be specific because the Universe has a sense of humor. Before I added the part about attracting 'people that I like being around' I was meeting some very interesting sorts."

After a few moments, the gathering was opened up for questions and answers.

"So, you recommend seeing a psychiatrist to do the healing," asked a small woman in the second row.

"No. I recommend working with someone, but it does not have to be a doctor. I chose to work with a certified therapist who was not licensed to administer drugs. Having been down that path before, and having had no success, I chose to try something different. I knew many of the things I needed to do to have the life I wanted, but I couldn't get past the resentment and regret. I didn't know how to heal; I didn't know how to release what I had been clinging to for so long--and I couldn't progress until I healed. For me, EMDR was the therapy that worked. Everyone is different; however, I encourage you to seek out a therapist who practices this treatment."

"When you did the EMDR, it really got you past all the fears and flashbacks from being with an abusive husband? I just can't seem to shake the nightmares." This question came from a woman in the first row.

"I still have rare moments that take me by surprise, and I still get scared sometimes. But yes, it really did get me past a lot of it; there was a time when I was afraid to close my eyes for fear of what sleep would bring, and one day the dreams just stopped. And, as it turned out, when we finally got to the topic of my ex-husband, I didn't need to revisit all that stuff. We started with the small issues and worked our way toward the most painful things. I did need to go in and clear out a multitude of regrets when it came to my son. However, because we had done all that work, I had had what the therapist called a 'universal healing.' When I brought up the scenes with my ex, there was no charge at all. It was just not an issue anymore."

"I'm afraid I won't be able to take care of myself and my children," came another comment from the group.

"First of all, I would replace that statement with, 'I know I can take care of myself and my children.' Picture yourself in your home; it's clean, warm, dry and safe. Your cabinets are full and your children are well fed and clothed. You don't have to know how it's going to happen; leave the details to the Universe. All you need to know, and *feel*, is that it is now a part of your future. Feel the gratitude--which is the force that catapults your dreams into reality--for what you know is already a part of your life, even if it has not yet manifested. It can be difficult if you're in the middle of a crappy situation. But feel the excitement as you make decisions about where you're going, not where you are presently. Honestly, there were times when fear kept me absolutely paralyzed. I was afraid of everything, but mostly, of being alone. So I clung to whoever I thought could save me from that awful fate, until the day when the outrage and pain of being mistreated became greater than my fear of solitude.

"Second, I have two words: power tools! My brother bought me a reciprocating saw for my fifty-second birthday. It was very empowering; before that day I didn't even know what a reciprocating saw was, let alone think I could use one. Now I know that, whether there's a guy around or not, I can have wood cut up for a nice cozy fire. I will never again let myself be trapped in a situation by thinking that I am incapable of doing something on my own. I envision myself tackling and completing the task, and feel how happy the success makes me. I got some power tools; read some handy-man books--and I know that I can do anything if I set my mind to it. Oh, and over the years, I've learned that just because someone charges a lot of money and says he knows what he's doing--doesn't make it so. I don't take anyone's word for anything; I do the research and then trust my gut.

"Okay, any more questions?" My lady smiled and glanced around at the women.

"Could you tell us a little more about how you manifest things?"

"Sure! Well, there are times when something involuntary begins to occupy my thoughts. If it's positive and makes me smile and feel good, I focus on it and encourage the image because I know it fits, it's already a part of my life.

"Other times, when I realize there is something I want, I express the desire to the Universe by saying, 'Thank you for bringing this into my life.' I grin and feel the gratitude and excitement of one receiving a gift because I know it will manifest. In the beginning I used an eight-inch lapis lazuli wand whenever I manifested. Lapis is a power stone; it helped me to channel my energy. Now I use it if I am distraught or feel the need for some extra help, but I'm perfectly capable of manifesting without it.

"Also, in the beginning, I worked on manifesting some cash. For the record, that doesn't work. I mean, I have an amount in my head and I know that, one day, my bank account statement will reflect that number. However, I found that just saying, 'Thank you for bringing me money,' was not making anything happen. Maybe because, on some level, I knew it would be worthless if I didn't earn it; but mostly, I really couldn't make my doubting-mind believe that the money would just materialize out of nowhere. So I changed my tactics and said, 'Thank you for making it possible for me to travel, or to build a homestead,' and so on. I found that then I began feeling a shift, and soon after I was inspired to write the book." She paused and took another sip of water, then added with a huge grin. "Today, I am living my dream."

"Excuse me, but what about negative thoughts? How do I keep them from happening?" A young woman piped up.

"Well, I still don't know how to keep them from happening, but I can tell you how I take away their power and make them disipate. Depending on the situation, I do one of two things. If I am able, I replace the thought with a happy, positive one each time it comes. However, if it's persistent and intense, and is causing me pain, I practice EMDR or one of the other tapping exercises taught to me by my therapist, and I also use 'four-two-six' breathing. That helps me a great deal; I just breathe in on a count of four, hold it for two, and let it out on a count of six. Fighting the thought doesn't work, because that will increase it's persistance because I am focusing on it--albeit trying to make it go away. I find it best to just acknowledge it, even thank the Universe for the heads-up, and either replace it or tap it away. Mind you, I practiced this treatment with the therapist for over a year before I ever felt the confidence to do it alone. If you have not been treated by a trained therapist, or the like, it is not advisable to just go home and start tapping on yourself. It is possible to reinforce negative thoughts and energy if you have no experience.

"Okay so, you all have the basic principles of how the law of attraction works. So just try this tonight: Quiet your mind and draw on a thought or image that brings you joy or gratitude. When you have the feeling say, 'People give me things,' with a big smile. Then conjur the joy of one receiving a gift and say thank you to the Universe, and smile as you go to sleep.

"I did that once, with results that made me giddy. I had been on the coast of California visiting some friends. Feeling particularly grateful and silly as I sat looking out over the bluffs, I stated that people give me things. The following day the young man at the hot tubs gave me a free soak; on day two my friend from Denmark gave me a pair of earrings out of the blue; and on the third day my other close friend gave me his scarf for no apparent reason.

"Or, you may want to be a bit more specific and, like they suggest in *The Secret*, you can manifest someone giving you a cup of coffee, or maybe something small that you wouldn't normally receive in an ordinary day. Don't make it far-fetched; make it something your doubting-mind can accept. The Universe does not judge; express what you want--and it begins to choreograph events so that your wish is fulfilled.

"When I began, if my confidence was lacking, I needed to imagine my dad walking into the Atlantic City convention center and sitting at that organ, when I'd manifest. I'd draw on the knowledge of what he did; after a while I was able to draw on my own experience for reinforcement.

"I'd like to close with a short gratitude list," my lady said when she was sure that there were no other questions.

"Whatever I am experiencing on any given day is preparing me for the next thing I will be doing, so I am grateful for all of it, positive and negative.

"I am grateful for all that has happened in my past and I would not change a thing, because it all made me who I am today, and I love that person.

"I am grateful for my family and friends and for my beautiful, best friend--Ebony." She leaned over and hugged me tightly and kissed me on the head.

"And lastly, I am so very grateful that I didn't pass out as I stood at that podium!" Everyone laughed before she added her final comment.

"Now that you know it's really up to you, before you go to bed tonight, look in the mirror and ask yourself this: What do you want your life to look like a year from today?"

It was a beautiful night as we said good-bye to everyone and walked out of the auditorium, and there were so many stars in the cloudless, black sky. After she gazed at them for a moment, my lady thanked the stars and we climbed into the truck. As she pulled out of the parking lot I snuggled close and put my head on her chest like I did when she sat on the floor of my cage so long ago. She smelled wonderful. There were no more cigarettes, no more festering hatred or fear, no more hormonal imbalance; there was nothing left to mask her true self. She hugged me back as I breathed in deeply, and I finally thought of the word I had been looking for.

"Home." She smells like *home*.

The End.

About the Author

*L*ori Ellen Brochhagen was raised in a small New Jersey suburb. With a high school diploma, she married and settled into being a wife and home maker but could not sit still for long. For this writer, the trek began in 1989, when she abruptly traded the white picket fence for a backpack and went out in search of who she really was. Using her black lab companion's perspective, Lori tells of some of her adventures as she learned, healed, grew strong, and found her truth.

Printed in the United States
By Bookmasters